Do-it-Yourself

HomeSchooling

POCKET

JOURNAL

60 Day Plan

WWW.FUNSCHOOLINGBOOKS.COM

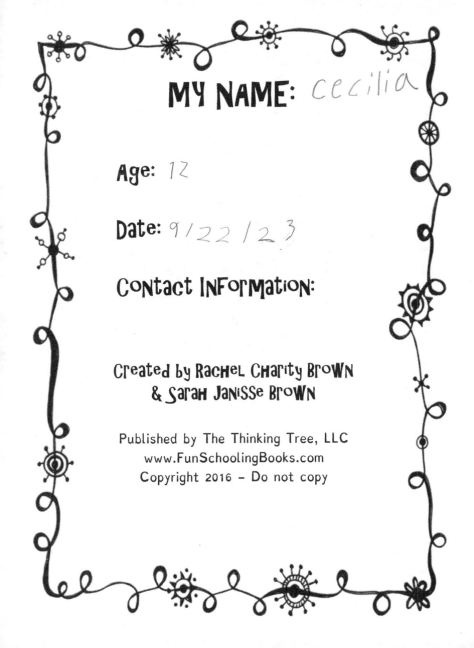

MY NAME: cecilia

Age: 12

Date: 9/22/23

Contact Information:

Created by Rachel Charity Brown
& Sarah Janisse Brown

What do you Want to Learn About?

1. sissts
2. spelling
3. mathc
4. reading
5. Histery

What do you Want to Accomplish this year?

1. with mathc
2. with spelling
3. with Histery
4. with reading
5.

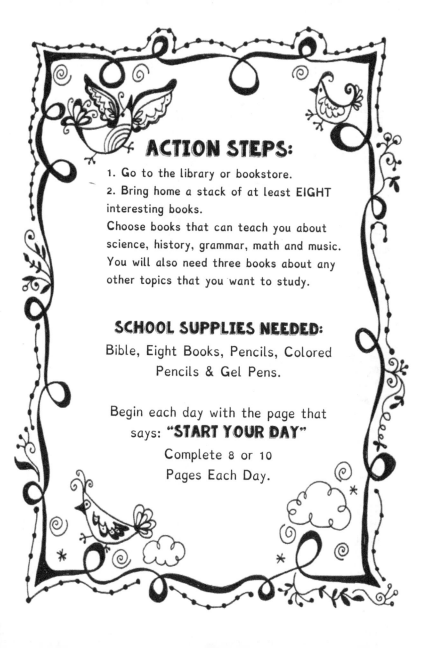

ACTION STEPS:

1. Go to the library or bookstore.
2. Bring home a stack of at least EIGHT interesting books.
Choose books that can teach you about science, history, grammar, math and music. You will also need three books about any other topics that you want to study.

SCHOOL SUPPLIES NEEDED:

Bible, Eight Books, Pencils, Colored Pencils & Gel Pens.

Begin each day with the page that says: **"START YOUR DAY"**
Complete 8 or 10 Pages Each Day.

Draw the cover of all your books!

Math

Grammar

Science

History

Read for at least one hour per day.

Music

START YOUR DAY!

DATE:
9/22/23

Today's News:

Nature Study

Draw something that God made.

Draw the Weather

To-Do List:
1. Play Barbie
2. Jo Gym
3. go Uth
4. go Home

How are you feeling today?

Bible Study Time

Prayer List:
1. For Daddy
2. For Mommy
3. and us)
4. to Feal
5. good again

Today's Bible Reading:

Bible Notes:

How can I serve others today?

Write a Bible Verse:

LEARN OR PRACTICE A SKILL

Goals:

Accomplishments:

MUSIC TIME

Use a Music Book
or Online Tutorial

Listening
Time

Enjoy an
Audio Book

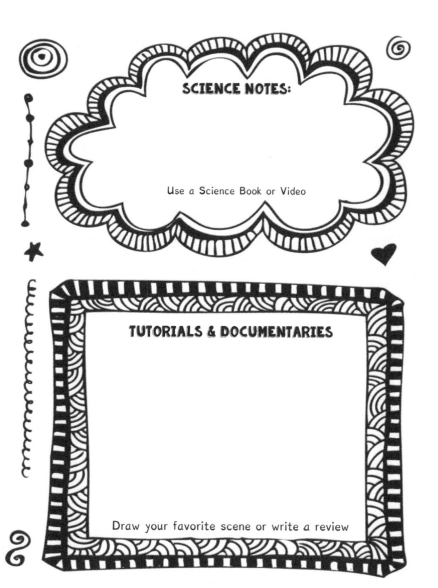

SCIENCE NOTES:

Use a Science Book or Video

TUTORIALS & DOCUMENTARIES

Draw your favorite scene or write a review

Grammar Lesson Notes:

Use Your Grammar Book

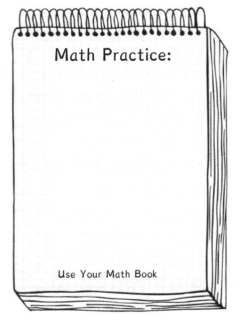

Math Practice:

Use Your Math Book

Spelling Words:

Make your Own Flash Cards (Front)

Make your Own Flash Cards (Back)

READING TIME

Spend time reading from all your books!
Copy your favorite paragraph:

Title:_____ Page Number_____

Illustrate It:

CREATIVE JOURNALING

Write a Poem, Song, Scripture or Story

I.Q. CHALLENGE- LOGIC GAMES

Use logic to draw the missing parts of the puzzle.

START YOUR DAY!

DATE:

_____

Today's News:

Nature Study

Draw something that God made.

Draw the Weather

To-Do List:

1.
2.
3.
4.

How are you feeling today?

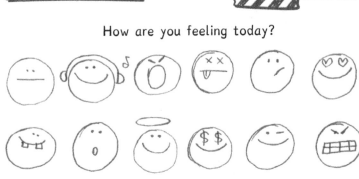

Bible Study Time

Prayer List:

1.
2.
3.
4.
5.

Today's Bible Reading:

Bible Notes:

How can I serve others today?

Write a Bible Verse:

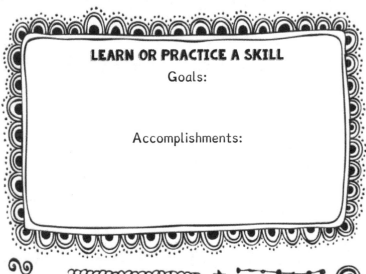

LEARN OR PRACTICE A SKILL

Goals:

Accomplishments:

MUSIC TIME

Use a Music Book
or Online Tutorial

Listening
Time

Enjoy an
Audio Book

I.Q. CHALLENGE- LOGIC GAMES

Use logic to draw the missing parts of the puzzle.

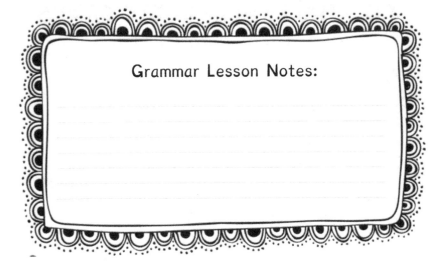

Grammar Lesson Notes:

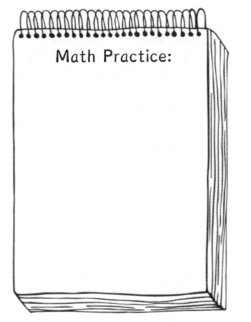

Math Practice:

Spelling Words:

Make your Own Flash Cards (Front)

Make your Own Flash Cards (Back)

READING TIME

Spend time reading from all your books!
Copy your favorite paragraph:

Title:_____ Page Number_____

_____
_____
_____
_____
_____
_____
_____
_____
_____
_____
_____
_____
_____
_____

Illustrate It:

START YOUR DAY!

DATE:

_____

Today's News:

Nature Study

Draw something that God made.

Draw the Weather

To-Do List:

1.
2.
3.
4.

How are you feeling today?

Bible Study Time

Prayer List:

1.
2.
3.
4.
5.

Today's Bible Reading:

Bible Notes:

How can I serve others today?

Write a Bible Verse:

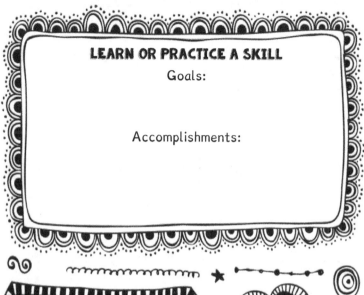

LEARN OR PRACTICE A SKILL

Goals:

Accomplishments:

MUSIC TIME

Listening Time

SCIENCE NOTES:

TUTORIALS & DOCUMENTARIES

Draw your favorite scene or write a review

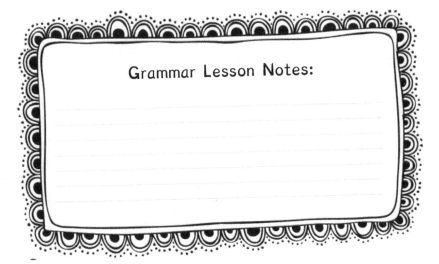

Grammar Lesson Notes:

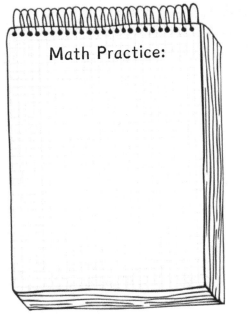

Math Practice:

Spelling Words:

Make your Own Flash Cards (Front)

Make your Own Flash Cards (Back)

READING TIME

Spend time reading from all your books!
Copy your favorite paragraph:

Title:_____ Page Number_____

CREATIVE JOURNALING

Write a Poem, Song, Scripture or Story

RELAX YOUR MIND

Listen to music or an audio book, while you color this illustration.
Use gel pens or colored pencils.

START YOUR DAY!

DATE:
_____
Today's News:

Nature Study

Draw something that God made.

Draw the Weather

To-Do List:

1.
2.
3.
4.

How are you feeling today?

Bible Study Time

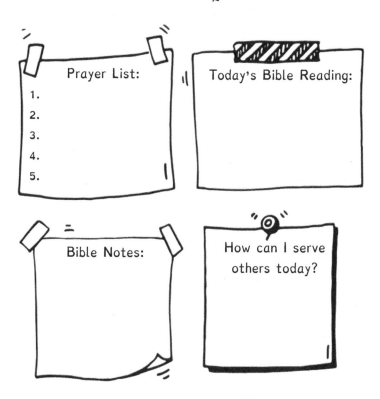

Prayer List:

1.
2.
3.
4.
5.

Today's Bible Reading:

Bible Notes:

How can I serve others today?

Write a Bible Verse:

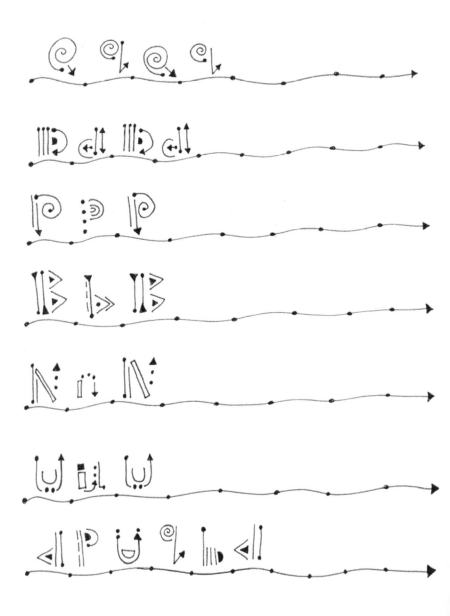

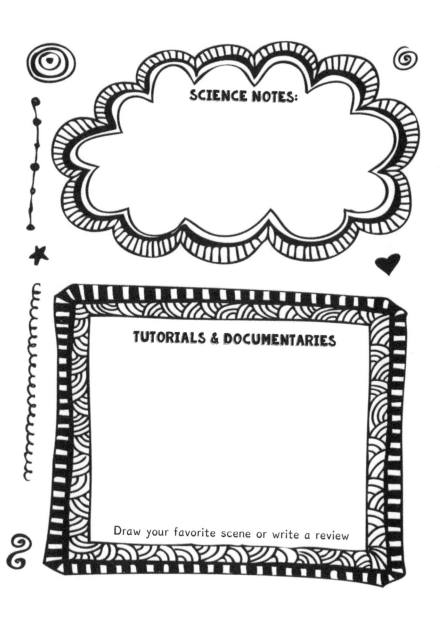

SCIENCE NOTES:

TUTORIALS & DOCUMENTARIES

Draw your favorite scene or write a review

Grammar Lesson Notes:

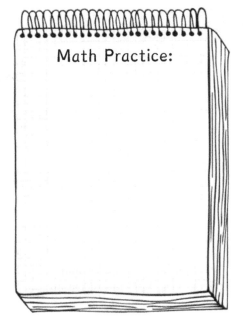

Math Practice:

Spelling Words:

Make your Own Flash Cards (Front)

Make your Own Flash Cards (Back)

READING TIME

Spend time reading from all your books!
Copy your favorite paragraph:

Title:_____ Page Number_____

CREATIVE JOURNALING

Write a Poem, Song, Scripture or Story

I.Q. CHALLENGE- LOGIC GAMES

Use logic to draw the missing parts of the puzzle.

START YOUR DAY!

DATE:
_____
Today's News:

Nature Study

Draw something that God made.

Draw the Weather

To-Do List:
1.
2.
3.
4.

How are you feeling today?

Bible Study Time

Prayer List:

1.
2.
3.
4.
5.

Today's Bible Reading:

Bible Notes:

How can I serve others today?

Write a Bible Verse:

LEARN OR PRACTICE A SKILL

Goals:

Accomplishments:

MUSIC TIME

Listening
Time

SCIENCE NOTES:

TUTORIALS & DOCUMENTARIES

Draw your favorite scene or write a review

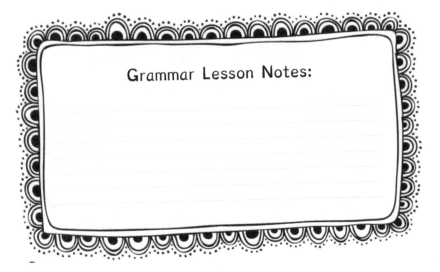

Grammar Lesson Notes:

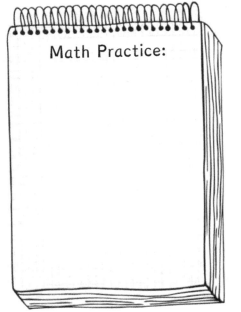

Math Practice:

Spelling Words:

Make your Own Flash Cards (Front)

Make your Own Flash Cards (Back)

READING TIME

Spend time reading from all your books!
Copy your favorite paragraph:

Title:_____ Page Number_____

CREATIVE JOURNALING

Write a Poem, Song, Scripture or Story

START YOUR DAY!

DATE:
_____
Today's News:

Nature Study

Draw something that God made.

Draw the Weather

To-Do List:
1.
2.
3.
4.

How are you feeling today?

Bible Study Time

Prayer List:
1.
2.
3.
4.
5.

Today's Bible Reading:

Bible Notes:

How can I serve others today?

Write a Bible Verse:

LEARN OR PRACTICE A SKILL

Goals:

Accomplishments:

MUSIC TIME

Listening
Time

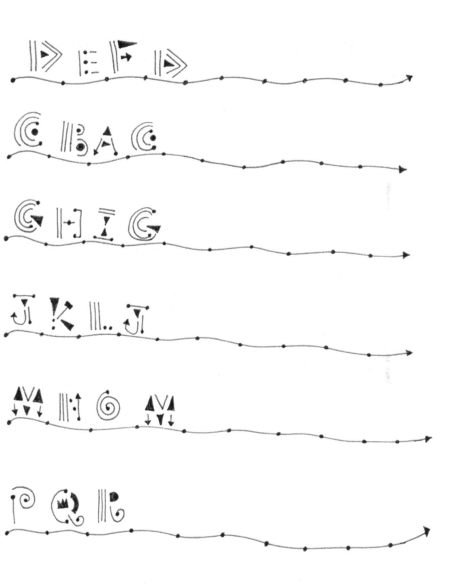

Grammar Lesson Notes:

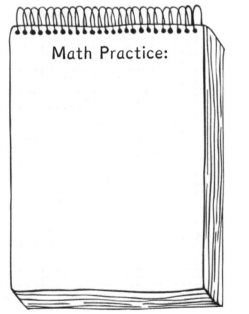

Math Practice:

Spelling Words:

Make your Own Flash Cards (Front)

Make your Own Flash Cards (Back)

READING TIME

Spend time reading from all your books!
Copy your favorite paragraph:

Title:_____ Page Number_____

CREATIVE JOURNALING

Write a Poem, Song, Scripture or Story

START YOUR DAY!

DATE:

_____

Today's News:

Nature Study

Draw something that God made.

Draw the Weather

To-Do List:
1.
2.
3.
4.

How are you feeling today?

Bible Study Time

Prayer List:

1.
2.
3.
4.
5.

Today's Bible Reading:

Bible Notes:

How can I serve others today?

Write a Bible Verse

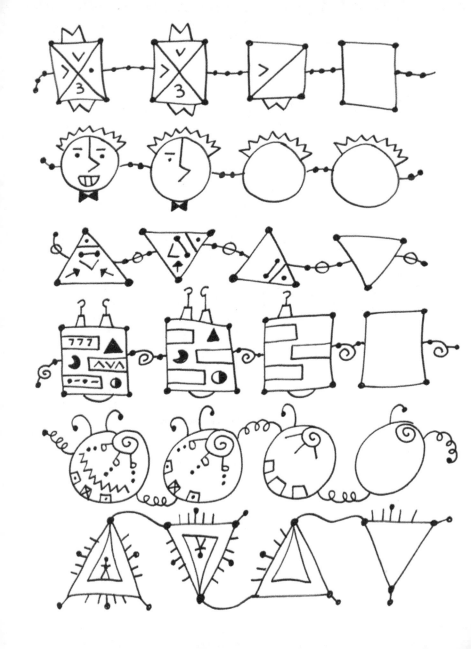

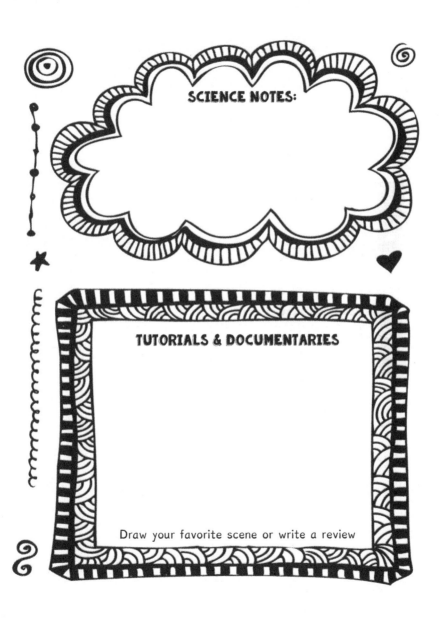

SCIENCE NOTES:

TUTORIALS & DOCUMENTARIES

Draw your favorite scene or write a review

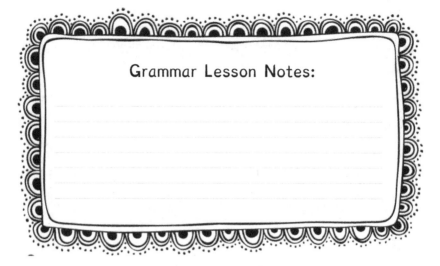

Grammar Lesson Notes:

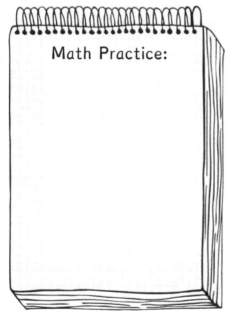

Math Practice:

Spelling Words:

Make your Own Flash Cards (Front)

Make your Own Flash Cards (Back)

READING TIME

Spend time reading from all your books!
Copy your favorite paragraph:

Title:_____ Page Number_____

CREATIVE JOURNALING

Write a Poem, Song, Scripture or Story

START YOUR DAY!

DATE:

_____

Today's News:

Nature Study

Draw something that God made.

Draw the Weather

To-Do List:

1.
2.
3.
4.

How are you feeling today?

Bible Study Time

Prayer List:

1.
2.
3.
4.
5.

Today's Bible Reading:

Bible Notes:

How can I serve others today?

Write a Bible Verse:

LEARN OR PRACTICE A SKILL

Goals:

Accomplishments:

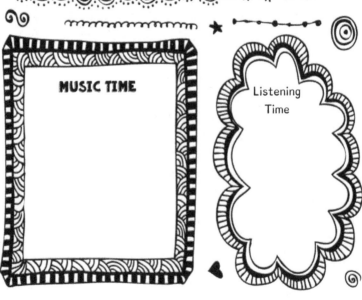

MUSIC TIME

Listening
Time

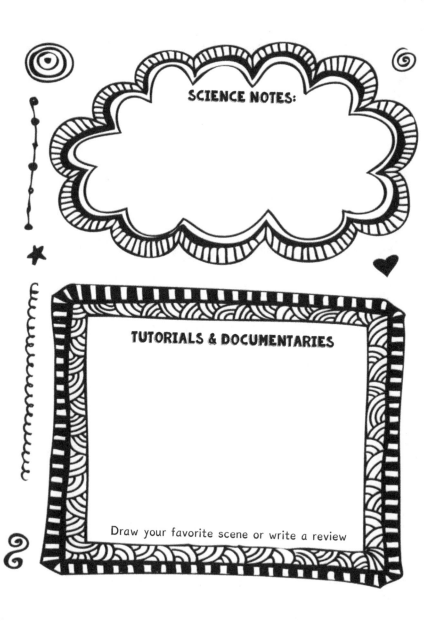

SCIENCE NOTES:

TUTORIALS & DOCUMENTARIES

Draw your favorite scene or write a review

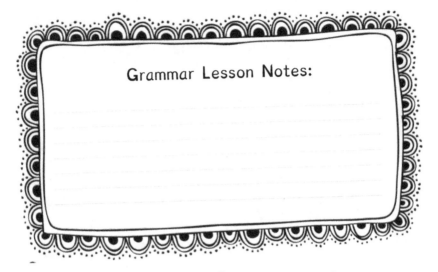

Grammar Lesson Notes:

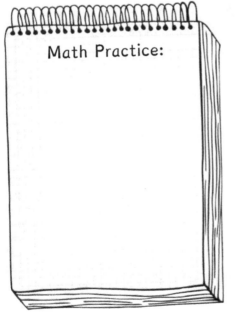

Math Practice:

Spelling Words:

Make your Own Flash Cards (Front)

Make your Own Flash Cards (Back)

READING TIME

Spend time reading from all your books!
Copy your favorite paragraph:

Title:_____ Page Number_____

CREATIVE JOURNALING

Write a Poem, Song, Scripture or Story

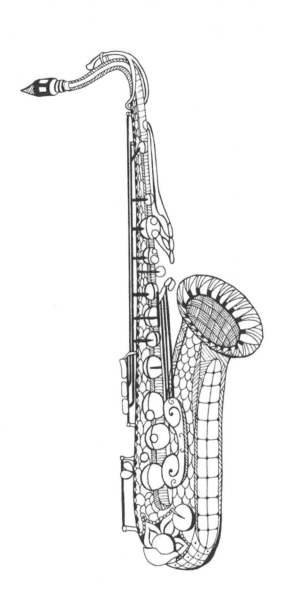

START YOUR DAY!

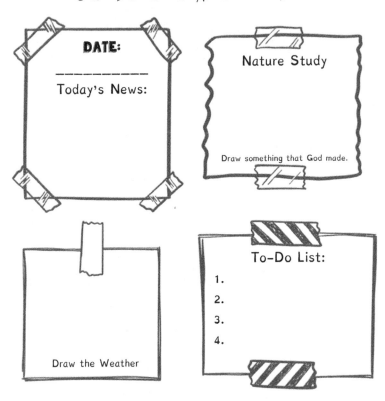

DATE:

_____

Today's News:

Nature Study

Draw something that God made.

Draw the Weather

To-Do List:

1.
2.
3.
4.

How are you feeling today?

Bible Study Time

Prayer List:
1.
2.
3.
4.
5.

Today's Bible Reading:

Bible Notes:

How can I serve others today?

Write a Bible Verse

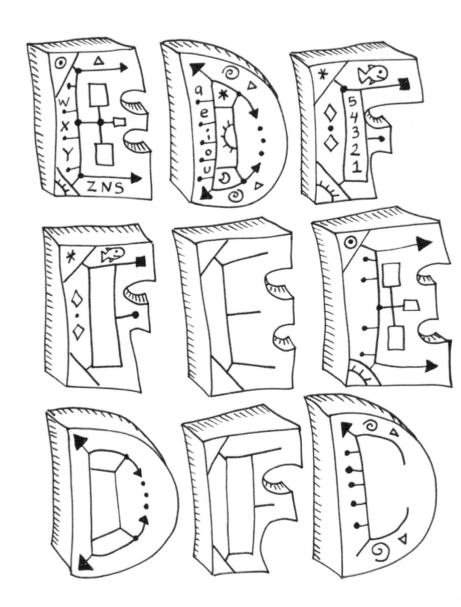

SCIENCE NOTES:

TUTORIALS & DOCUMENTARIES

Draw your favorite scene or write a review

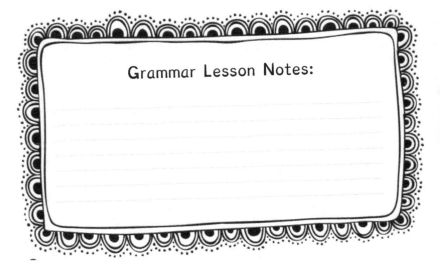

Grammar Lesson Notes:

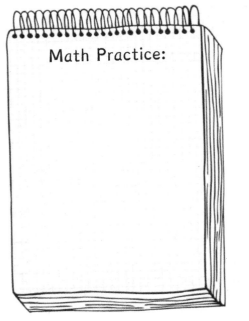

Math Practice:

Spelling Words:

Make your Own Flash Cards (Front)

Make your Own Flash Cards (Back)

READING TIME

Spend time reading from all your books!
Copy your favorite paragraph:

Title:_____ Page Number_____

CREATIVE JOURNALING

Write a Poem, Song, Scripture or Story

START YOUR DAY!

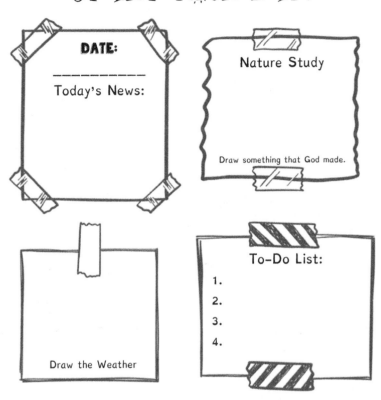

DATE:

_____

Today's News:

Nature Study

Draw something that God made.

Draw the Weather

To-Do List:

1.
2.
3.
4.

How are you feeling today?

Bible Study Time

Prayer List:

1.
2.
3.
4.
5.

Today's Bible Reading:

Bible Notes:

How can I serve others today?

Write a Bible Verse:

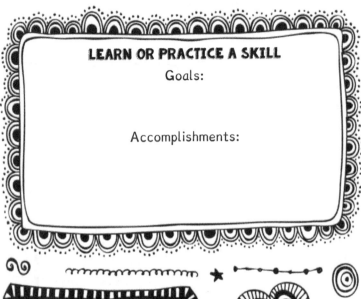

LEARN OR PRACTICE A SKILL

Goals:

Accomplishments:

MUSIC TIME

Listening
Time

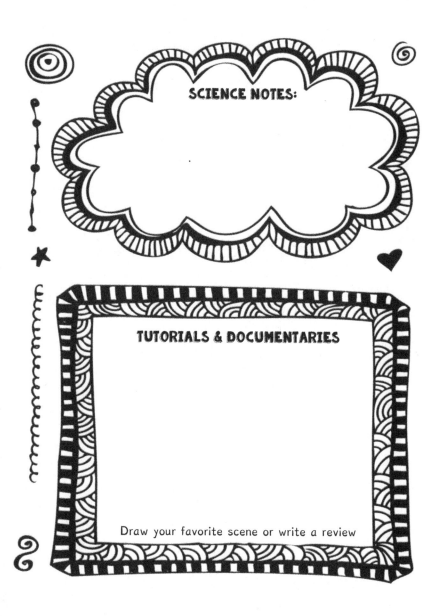

SCIENCE NOTES:

TUTORIALS & DOCUMENTARIES

Draw your favorite scene or write a review

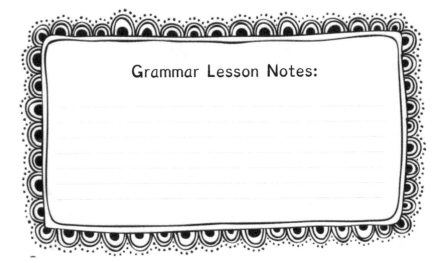

Grammar Lesson Notes:

Math Practice:

Spelling Words:

Make your Own Flash Cards (Front)

Make your Own Flash Cards (Back)

READING TIME

Spend time reading from all your books!
Copy your favorite paragraph:

Title:_____ Page Number_____

CREATIVE JOURNALING

Write a Poem, Song, Scripture or Story

START YOUR DAY!

DATE:

_____

Today's News:

Nature Study

Draw something that God made.

Draw the Weather

To-Do List:

1.
2.
3.
4.

How are you feeling today?

Bible Study Time

Prayer List:

1.
2.
3.
4.
5.

Today's Bible Reading:

Bible Notes:

How can I serve others today?

Write a Bible Verse:

LEARN OR PRACTICE A SKILL

Goals:

Accomplishments:

MUSIC TIME

Listening
Time

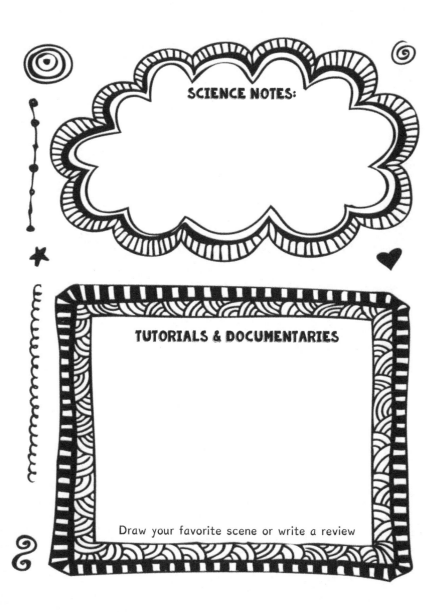

SCIENCE NOTES:

TUTORIALS & DOCUMENTARIES

Draw your favorite scene or write a review

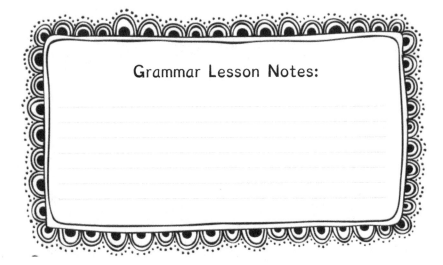

Grammar Lesson Notes:

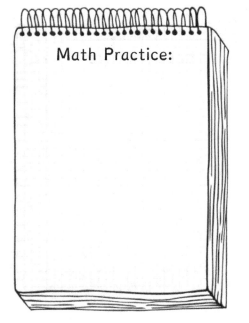

Math Practice:

Spelling Words:

Make your Own Flash Cards (Front)

Make your Own Flash Cards (Back)

READING TIME

Spend time reading from all your books!
Copy your favorite paragraph:

Title:_____ Page Number_____

_____
_____
_____
_____
_____
_____
_____
_____
_____
_____
_____
_____
_____
_____

CREATIVE JOURNALING

Write a Poem, Song, Scripture or Story

START YOUR DAY!

DATE:

_____

Today's News:

Nature Study

Draw something that God made.

Draw the Weather

To-Do List:

1.
2.
3.
4.

How are you feeling today?

Bible Study Time

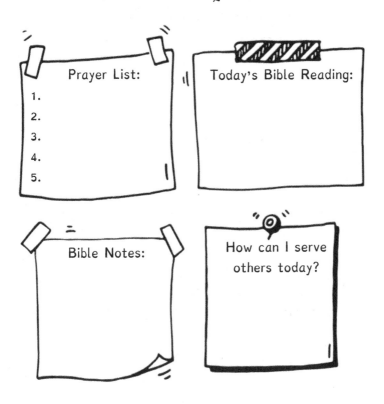

Prayer List:

1.
2.
3.
4.
5.

Today's Bible Reading:

Bible Notes:

How can I serve others today?

Write a Bible Verse:

LEARN OR PRACTICE A SKILL

Goals:

Accomplishments:

MUSIC TIME

Listening
Time

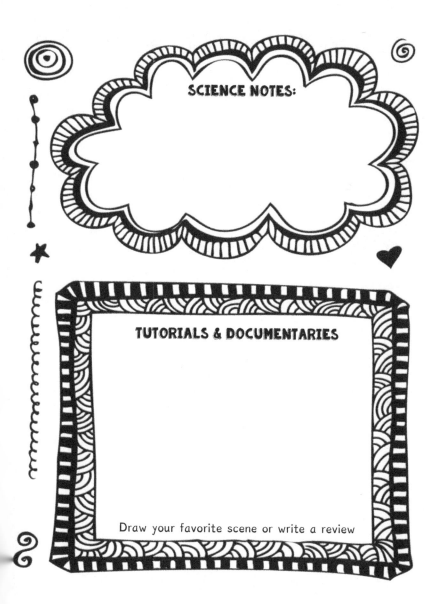

SCIENCE NOTES:

TUTORIALS & DOCUMENTARIES

Draw your favorite scene or write a review

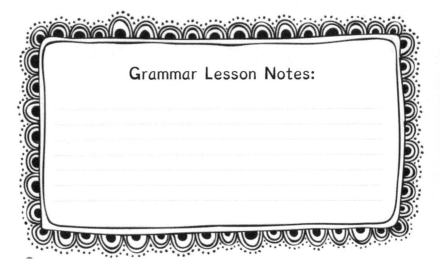

Grammar Lesson Notes:

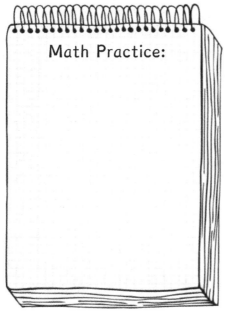

Math Practice:

Spelling Words:

Make your Own Flash Cards (Front)

Make your Own Flash Cards (Back)

READING TIME

Spend time reading from all your books!
Copy your favorite paragraph:

Title:_____ Page Number_____

_____
_____
_____
_____
_____
_____
_____
_____
_____
_____
_____
_____
_____
_____
_____

Illustrate It:

CREATIVE JOURNALING

Write a Poem, Song, Scripture or Story

START YOUR DAY!

DATE:

_____

Today's News:

Nature Study

Draw something that God made.

Draw the Weather

To-Do List:

1.
2.
3.
4.

How are you feeling today?

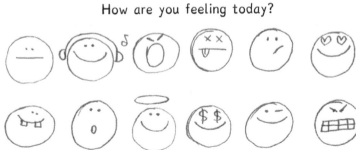

Bible Study Time

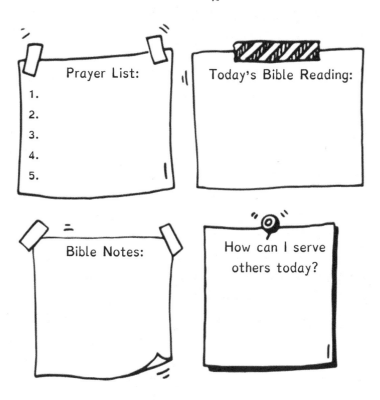

Prayer List:

1.
2.
3.
4.
5.

Today's Bible Reading:

Bible Notes:

How can I serve others today?

Write a Bible Verse:

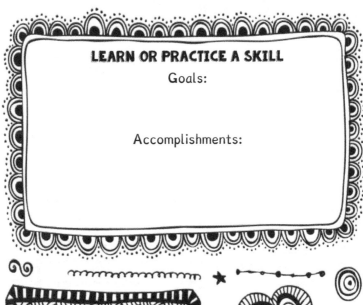

LEARN OR PRACTICE A SKILL

Goals:

Accomplishments:

MUSIC TIME

Listening
Time

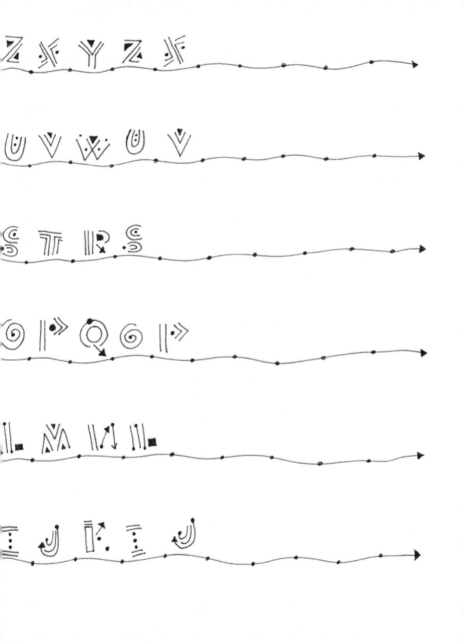

Grammar Lesson Notes:

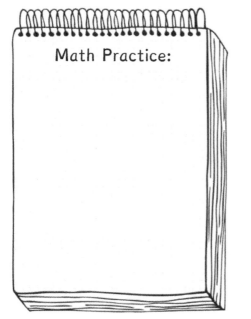

Math Practice:

Spelling Words:

Make your Own Flash Cards (Front)

Make your Own Flash Cards (Back)

READING TIME

Spend time reading from all your books!
Copy your favorite paragraph:

Title:_____ Page Number_____

CREATIVE JOURNALING

Write a Poem, Song, Scripture or Story

START YOUR DAY!

DATE:

_____

Today's News:

Nature Study

Draw something that God made.

Draw the Weather

To-Do List:

1.
2.
3.
4.

How are you feeling today?

Bible Study Time

Prayer List:
1.
2.
3.
4.
5.

Today's Bible Reading:

Bible Notes:

How can I serve others today?

Write a Bible Verse:

LEARN OR PRACTICE A SKILL

Goals:

Accomplishments:

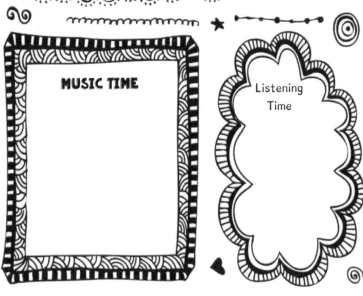

MUSIC TIME

Listening
Time

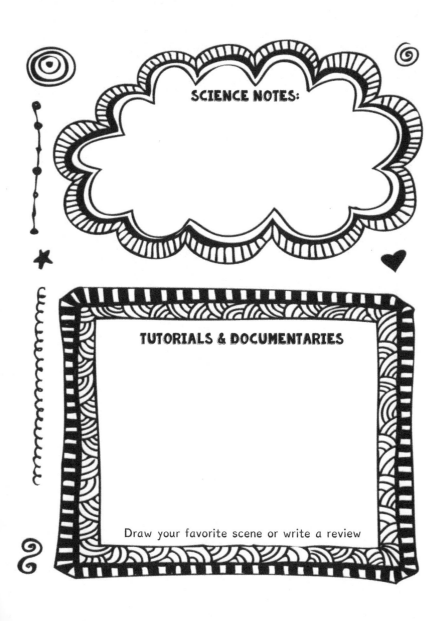

SCIENCE NOTES:

TUTORIALS & DOCUMENTARIES

Draw your favorite scene or write a review

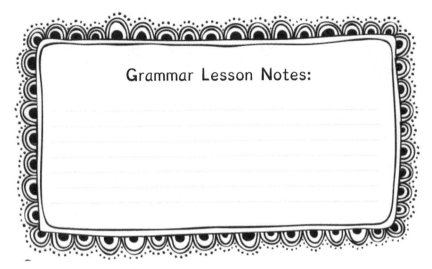

Grammar Lesson Notes:

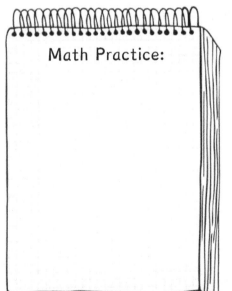

Math Practice:

Spelling Words:

Make your Own Flash Cards (Front)

Make your Own Flash Cards (Back)

READING TIME

Spend time reading from all your books!
Copy your favorite paragraph:

Title:_____ Page Number_____

Illustrate It:

CREATIVE JOURNALING

Write a Poem, Song, Scripture or Story

START YOUR DAY!

DATE:
_____
Today's News:

Nature Study

Draw something that God made.

Draw the Weather

To-Do List:

1.
2.
3.
4.

How are you feeling today?

Bible Study Time

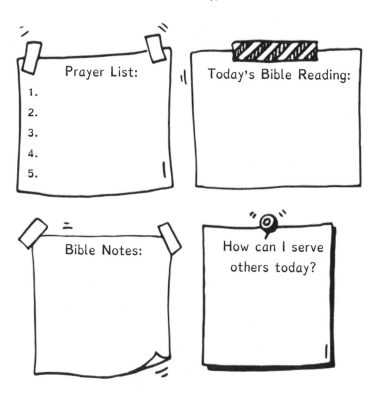

Prayer List:

1.
2.
3.
4.
5.

Today's Bible Reading:

Bible Notes:

How can I serve others today?

Write a Bible Verse:

LEARN OR PRACTICE A SKILL

Goals:

Accomplishments:

MUSIC TIME

Listening
Time

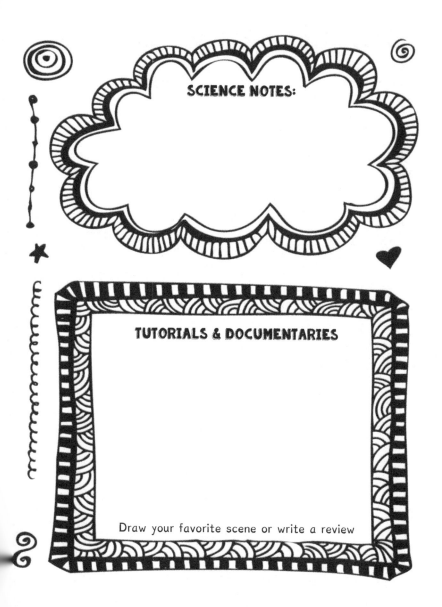

SCIENCE NOTES:

TUTORIALS & DOCUMENTARIES

Draw your favorite scene or write a review

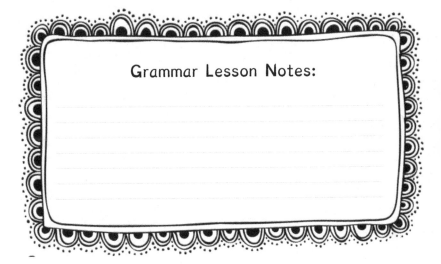

Grammar Lesson Notes:

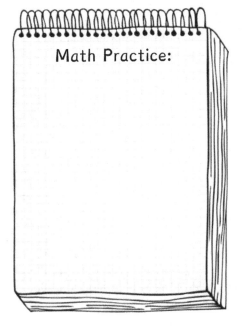

Math Practice:

Spelling Words:

Make your Own Flash Cards (Front)

Make your Own Flash Cards (Back)

READING TIME

Spend time reading from all your books!
Copy your favorite paragraph:

Title:_____ Page Number_____

_____

_____

_____

_____

_____

_____

_____

_____

_____

_____

_____

_____

_____

_____

_____

Illustrate It:

CREATIVE JOURNALING

Write a Poem, Song, Scripture or Story

START YOUR DAY!

DATE:

_____

Today's News:

Nature Study

Draw something that God made.

Draw the Weather

To-Do List:
1.
2.
3.
4.

How are you feeling today?

Bible Study Time

Prayer List:

1.
2.
3.
4.
5.

Today's Bible Reading:

Bible Notes:

How can I serve others today?

Write a Bible Verse:

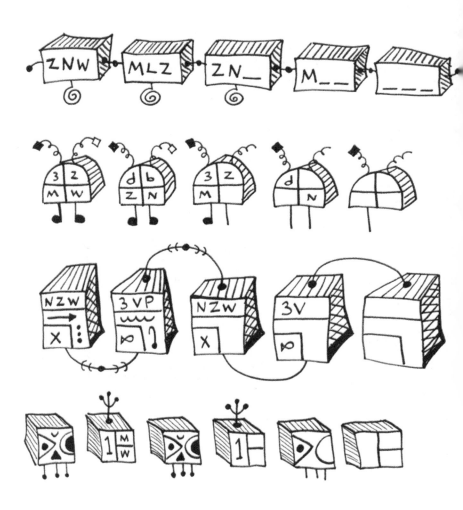

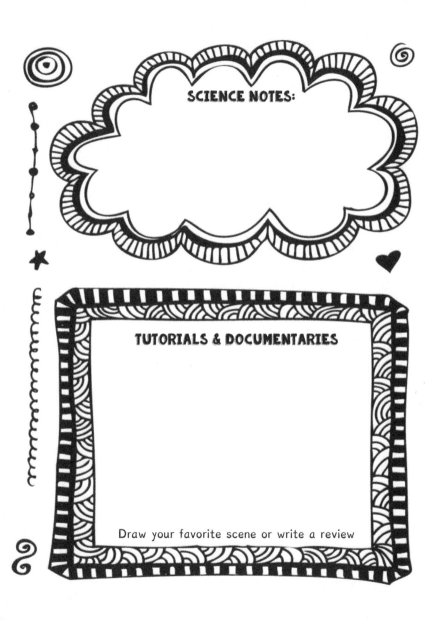

SCIENCE NOTES:

TUTORIALS & DOCUMENTARIES

Draw your favorite scene or write a review

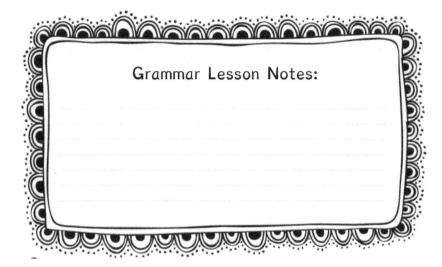

Grammar Lesson Notes:

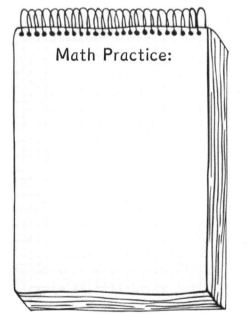

Math Practice:

Spelling Words:

Make your Own Flash Cards (Front)

Make your Own Flash Cards (Back)

READING TIME

Spend time reading from all your books!
Copy your favorite paragraph:

Title:_____ Page Number_____

CREATIVE JOURNALING

Write a Poem, Song, Scripture or Story

START YOUR DAY!

DATE:

_____

Today's News:

Nature Study

Draw something that God made.

Draw the Weather

To-Do List:

1.
2.
3.
4.

How are you feeling today?

Bible Study Time

Prayer List:

1.
2.
3.
4.
5.

Today's Bible Reading:

Bible Notes:

How can I serve others today?

Write a Bible Verse:

LEARN OR PRACTICE A SKILL

Goals:

Accomplishments:

MUSIC TIME

Listening
Time

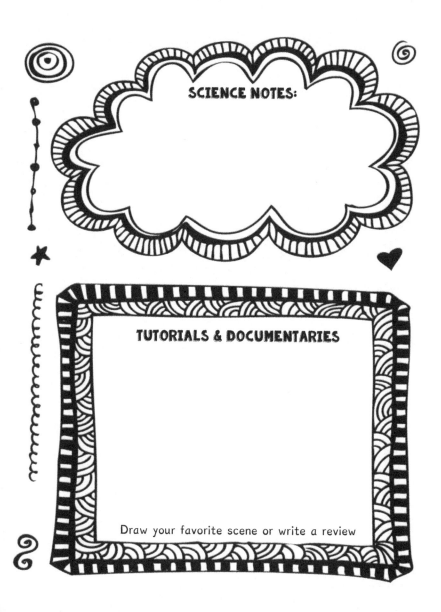

SCIENCE NOTES:

TUTORIALS & DOCUMENTARIES

Draw your favorite scene or write a review

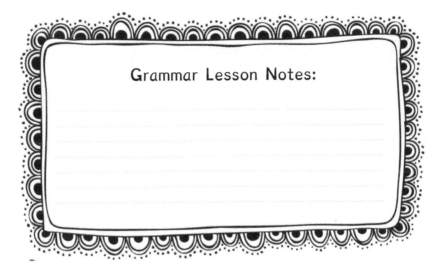

Grammar Lesson Notes:

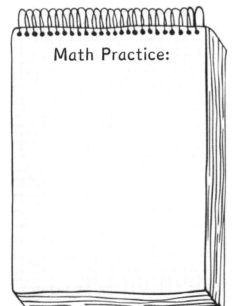

Math Practice:

Spelling Words:

Make your Own Flash Cards (Front)

Make your Own Flash Cards (Back)

READING TIME

Spend time reading from all your books!
Copy your favorite paragraph:

Title:_____ Page Number_____

Illu

CREATIVE JOURNALING

Write a Poem, Song, Scripture or Story

START YOUR DAY!

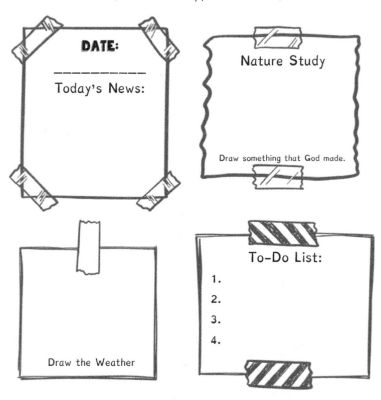

DATE:

_____

Today's News:

Nature Study

Draw something that God made.

Draw the Weather

To-Do List:

1.

2.

3.

4.

How are you feeling today?

Bible Study Time

Prayer List:

1.
2.
3.
4.
5.

Today's Bible Reading:

Bible Notes:

How can I serve
others today?

Write a Bible Verse:

LEARN OR PRACTICE A SKILL

Goals:

Accomplishments:

MUSIC TIME

Listening
Time

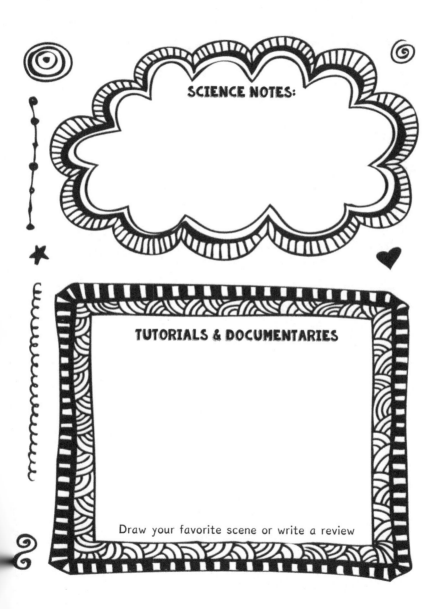

SCIENCE NOTES:

TUTORIALS & DOCUMENTARIES

Draw your favorite scene or write a review

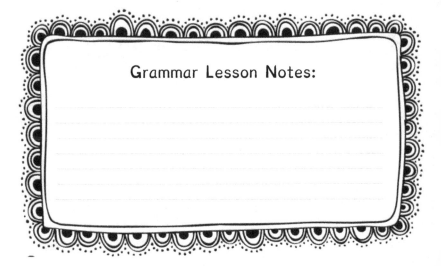

Grammar Lesson Notes:

Spelling Words:

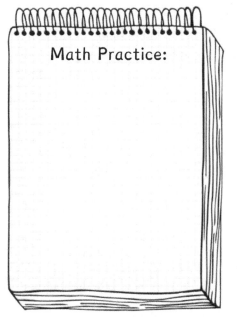

Math Practice:

Make your Own Flash Cards (Front)

Make your Own Flash Cards (Back)

READING TIME

Spend time reading from all your books!
Copy your favorite paragraph:

Title:_____ Page Number_____

_____
_____
_____
_____
_____
_____
_____
_____
_____
_____
_____
_____
_____

Illustrate It:

CREATIVE JOURNALING

Write a Poem, Song, Scripture or Story

START YOUR DAY!

DATE:

_____

Today's News:

Nature Study

Draw something that God made.

Draw the Weather

To-Do List:

1.
2.
3.
4.

How are you feeling today?

Bible Study Time

Prayer List:

1.
2.
3.
4.
5.

Today's Bible Reading:

Bible Notes:

How can I serve others today?

Write a Bible Verse:

LEARN OR PRACTICE A SKILL

Goals:

Accomplishments:

MUSIC TIME

Listening
Time

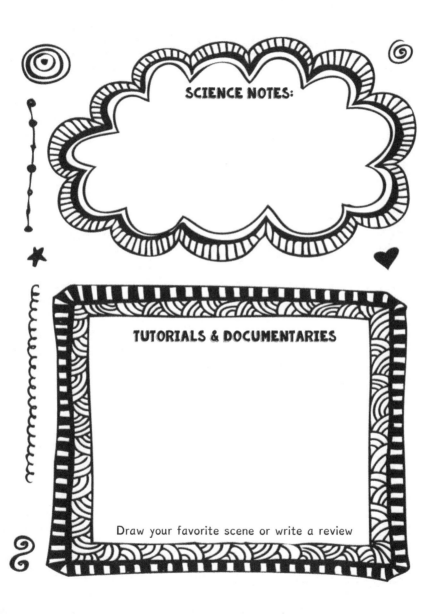

SCIENCE NOTES:

TUTORIALS & DOCUMENTARIES

Draw your favorite scene or write a review

Grammar Lesson Notes:

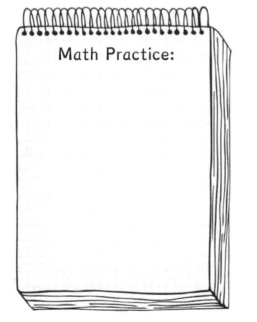

Math Practice:

Spelling Words:

Make your Own Flash Cards (Front)

Make your Own Flash Cards (Back)

READING TIME

Spend time reading from all your books!
Copy your favorite paragraph:
Notes

Title:_____ Page Number_____

I

CREATIVE JOURNALING

Write a Poem, Song, Scripture or Story

START YOUR DAY!

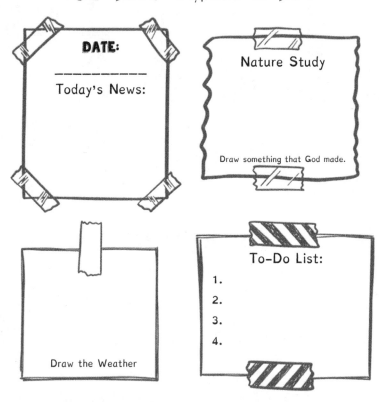

DATE:

_____

Today's News:

Nature Study

Draw something that God made.

Draw the Weather

To-Do List:

1.
2.
3.
4.

How are you feeling today?

Bible Study Time

Prayer List:

1.
2.
3.
4.
5.

Today's Bible Reading:

Bible Notes:

How can I serve others today?

Write a Bible Verse:

LEARN OR PRACTICE A SKILL

Goals:

Accomplishments:

MUSIC TIME

Listening
Time

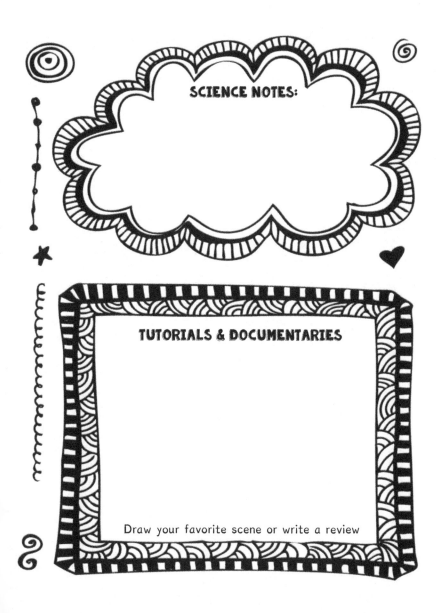

SCIENCE NOTES:

TUTORIALS & DOCUMENTARIES

Draw your favorite scene or write a review

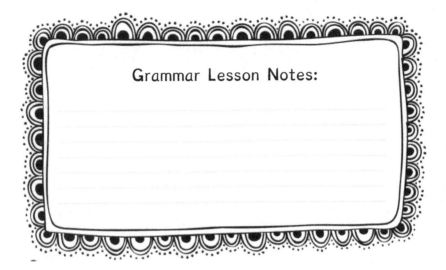

Grammar Lesson Notes:

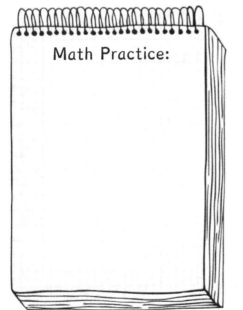

Math Practice:

Spelling Words:

Make your Own Flash Cards (Front)

Make your Own Flash Cards (Back)

READING TIME

Spend time reading from all your books!

Copy your favorite paragraph:

Notes

Title:_____ Page Number_____

Ilustrate It:

CREATIVE JOURNALING

Write a Poem, Song, Scripture or Story

START YOUR DAY!

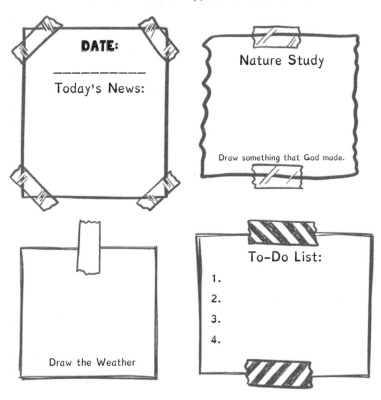

DATE:
_____

Today's News:

Nature Study

Draw something that God made.

Draw the Weather

To-Do List:

1.
2.
3.
4.

How are you feeling today?

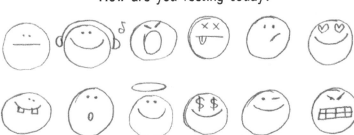

Bible Study Time

Prayer List:

1.
2.
3.
4.
5.

Today's Bible Reading:

Bible Notes:

How can I serve others today?

Write a Bible Verse:

LEARN OR PRACTICE A SKILL

Goals:

Accomplishments:

MUSIC TIME

Listening
Time

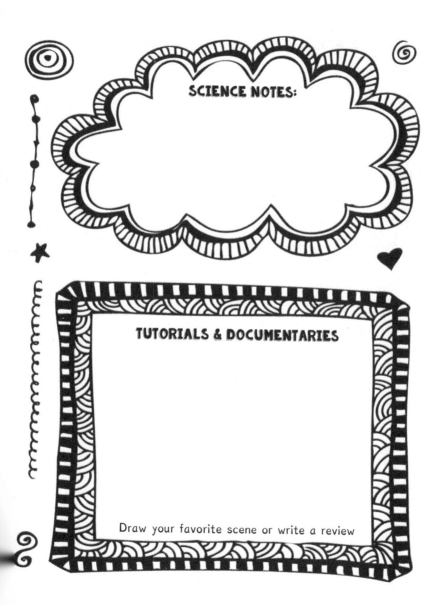

SCIENCE NOTES:

TUTORIALS & DOCUMENTARIES

Draw your favorite scene or write a review

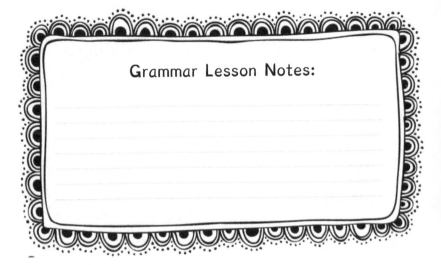

Grammar Lesson Notes:

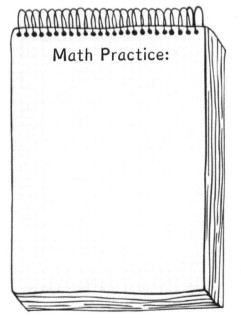

Math Practice:

Spelling Words:

Make your Own Flash Cards (Front)

Make your Own Flash Cards (Back)

READING TIME

Spend time reading from all your books!
Copy your favorite paragraph:

Notes

Title:_____ Page Number_____

_____

_____

_____

_____

_____

_____

_____

_____

_____

_____

_____

_____

Illustrate It:

CREATIVE JOURNALING

Write a Poem, Song, Scripture or Story

START YOUR DAY!

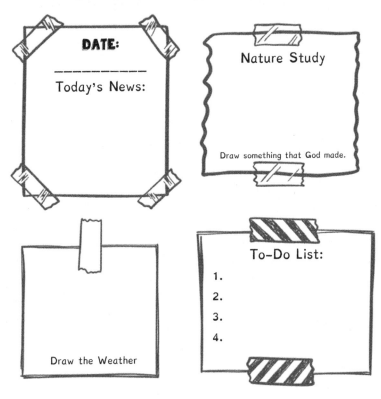

DATE:

_____

Today's News:

Nature Study

Draw something that God made.

Draw the Weather

To-Do List:

1.
2.
3.
4.

How are you feeling today?

Bible Study Time

Prayer List:

1.
2.
3.
4.
5.

Today's Bible Reading:

Bible Notes:

How can I serve others today?

Write a Bible Verse:

LEARN OR PRACTICE A SKILL

Goals:

Accomplishments:

MUSIC TIME

Listening
Time

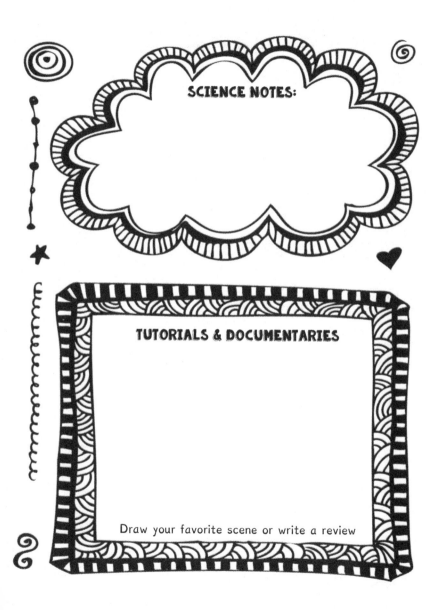

SCIENCE NOTES:

TUTORIALS & DOCUMENTARIES

Draw your favorite scene or write a review

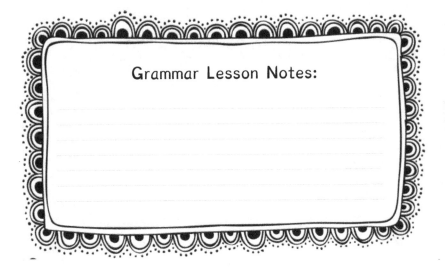

Grammar Lesson Notes:

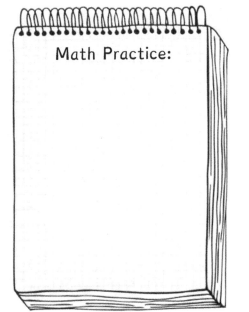

Math Practice:

Spelling Words:

Make your Own Flash Cards (Front)

Make your Own Flash Cards (Back)

READING TIME

Spend time reading from all your books!

Copy your favorite paragraph:

Notes

Title:_____ Page Number_____

CREATIVE JOURNALING

Write a Poem, Song, Scripture or Story

START YOUR DAY!

DATE:

_____

Today's News:

Nature Study

Draw something that God made.

Draw the Weather

To-Do List:

1.
2.
3.
4.

How are you feeling today?

Bible Study Time

Prayer List:

1.
2.
3.
4.
5.

Today's Bible Reading:

Bible Notes:

How can I serve others today?

Write a Bible Verse:

LEARN OR PRACTICE A SKILL

Goals:

Accomplishments:

MUSIC TIME

Listening
Time

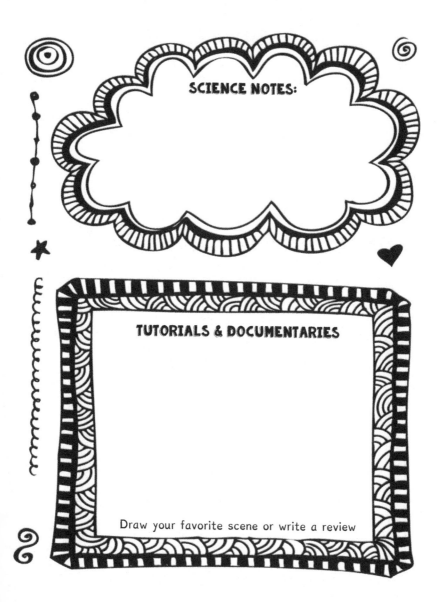

SCIENCE NOTES:

TUTORIALS & DOCUMENTARIES

Draw your favorite scene or write a review

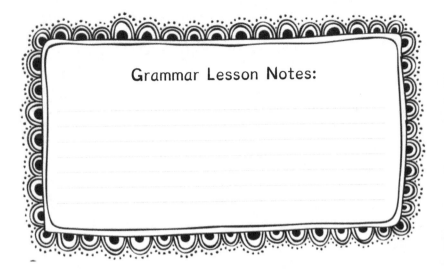

Grammar Lesson Notes:

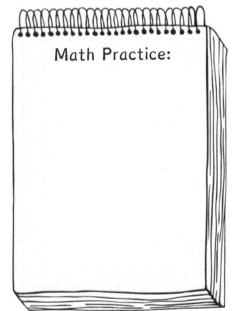

Math Practice:

Spelling Words:

Make your Own Flash Cards (Front)

Make your Own Flash Cards (Back)

READING TIME

Spend time reading from all your books!

Copy your favorite paragraph:

Notes

Title:_____ Page Number_____

CREATIVE JOURNALING

Write a Poem, Song, Scripture or Story

START YOUR DAY!

DATE:

_____

Today's News:

Nature Study

Draw something that God made.

Draw the Weather

To-Do List:

1.
2.
3.
4.

How are you feeling today?

Bible Study Time

Prayer List:

1.
2.
3.
4.
5.

Today's Bible Reading:

Bible Notes:

How can I serve others today?

Write a Bible Verse

LEARN OR PRACTICE A SKILL

Goals:

Accomplishments:

MUSIC TIME

Listening
Time

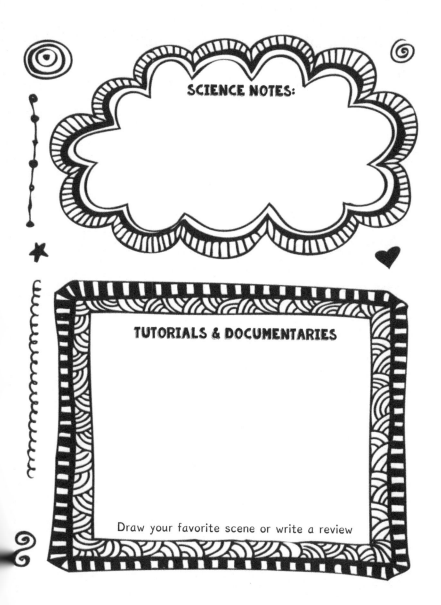

SCIENCE NOTES:

TUTORIALS & DOCUMENTARIES

Draw your favorite scene or write a review

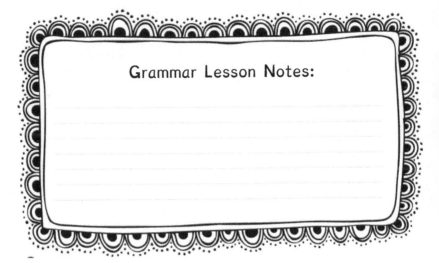

Grammar Lesson Notes:

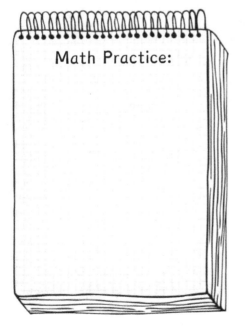

Math Practice:

Spelling Words:

Make your Own Flash Cards (Front)

Make your Own Flash Cards (Back)

READING TIME

Spend time reading from all your books!

Copy your favorite paragraph:

Notes

Title:_____ Page Number_____

CREATIVE JOURNALING

Write a Poem, Song, Scripture or Story

START YOUR DAY!

DATE:

_____

Today's News:

Nature Study

Draw something that God made.

Draw the Weather

To-Do List:

1.
2.
3.
4.

How are you feeling today?

Bible Study Time

Prayer List:

1.
2.
3.
4.
5.

Today's Bible Reading:

Bible Notes:

How can I serve others today?

Write a Bible Verse:

LEARN OR PRACTICE A SKILL

Goals:

Accomplishments:

MUSIC TIME

Listening
Time

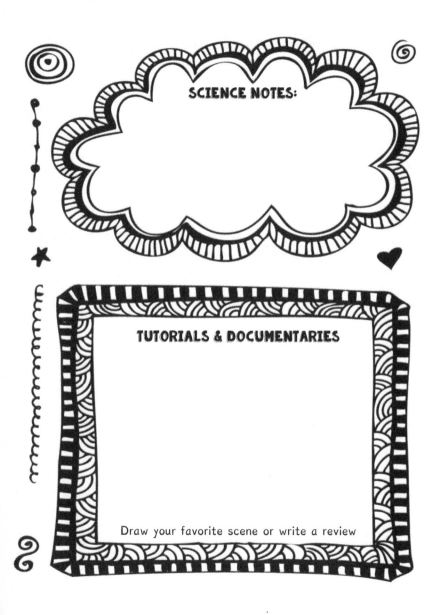

SCIENCE NOTES:

TUTORIALS & DOCUMENTARIES

Draw your favorite scene or write a review

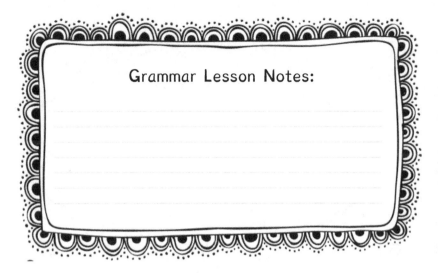

Grammar Lesson Notes:

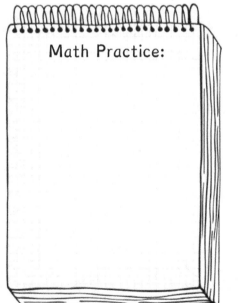

Math Practice:

Spelling Words:

Make your Own Flash Cards (Front)

Make your Own Flash Cards (Back)

READING TIME

Spend time reading from all your books!

Copy your favorite paragraph:

Notes

Title:_____ Page Number_____

CREATIVE JOURNALING

Write a Poem, Song, Scripture or Story

START YOUR DAY!

DATE:

_____

Today's News:

Nature Study

Draw something that God made.

Draw the Weather

To-Do List:

1.
2.
3.
4.

How are you feeling today?

Bible Study Time

Prayer List:
1.
2.
3.
4.
5.

Today's Bible Reading:

Bible Notes:

How can I serve others today?

Write a Bible Verse:

LEARN OR PRACTICE A SKILL

Goals:

Accomplishments:

MUSIC TIME

Listening
Time

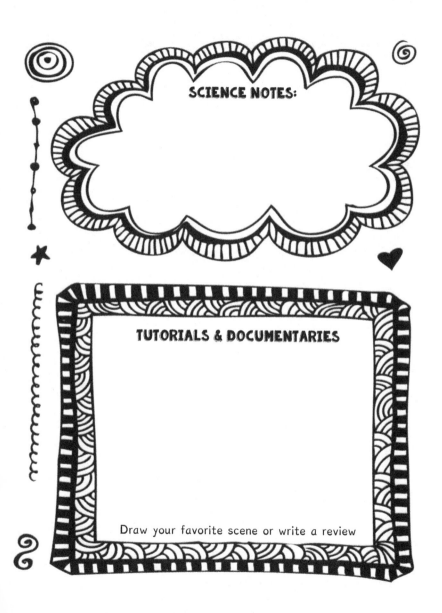

SCIENCE NOTES:

TUTORIALS & DOCUMENTARIES

Draw your favorite scene or write a review

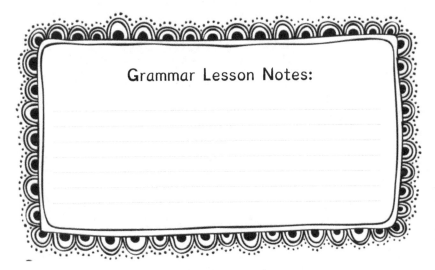

Grammar Lesson Notes:

Spelling Words:

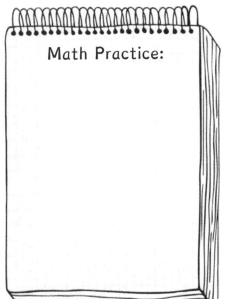

Math Practice:

Make your Own Flash Cards (Front)

Make your Own Flash Cards (Back)

READING TIME

Spend time reading from all your books!

Copy your favorite paragraph:

Notes

Title:_____ Page Number_____

CREATIVE JOURNALING

Write a Poem, Song, Scripture or Story

START YOUR DAY!

DATE:

_____

Today's News:

Nature Study

Draw something that God made.

Draw the Weather

To-Do List:

1.
2.
3.
4.

How are you feeling today?

Bible Study Time

Prayer List:

1.
2.
3.
4.
5.

Today's Bible Reading:

Bible Notes:

How can I serve others today?

Write a Bible Verse:

LEARN OR PRACTICE A SKILL

Goals:

Accomplishments:

MUSIC TIME

Listening
Time

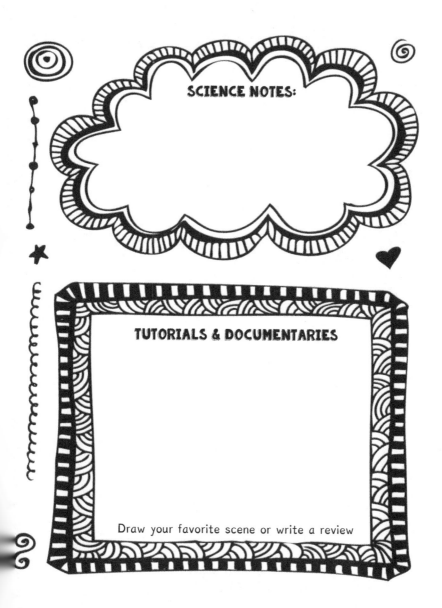

SCIENCE NOTES:

TUTORIALS & DOCUMENTARIES

Draw your favorite scene or write a review

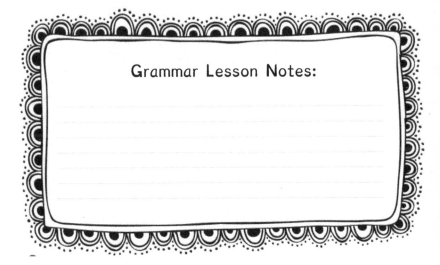

Grammar Lesson Notes:

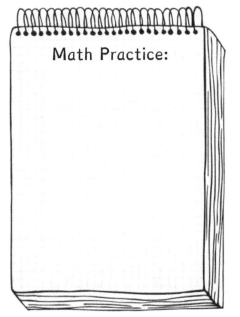

Math Practice:

Spelling Words:

Make your Own Flash Cards (Front)

Make your Own Flash Cards (Back)

READING TIME

Spend time reading from all your books!

Copy your favorite paragraph:

Notes

Title:_____ Page Number_____

_____

_____

_____

_____

_____

_____

_____

_____

_____

_____

_____

_____

_____

_____

Illustrate It:

CREATIVE JOURNALING

Write a Poem, Song, Scripture or Story

START YOUR DAY!

DATE:

_____

Today's News:

Nature Study

Draw something that God made.

Draw the Weather

To-Do List:

1.
2.
3.
4.

How are you feeling today?

Bible Study Time

Prayer List:

1.
2.
3.
4.
5.

Today's Bible Reading:

Bible Notes:

How can I serve others today?

Write a Bible Verse

CREATIVE JOURNALING

Write a Poem, Song, Scripture or Story

LEARN OR PRACTICE A SKILL

Goals:

Accomplishments:

MUSIC TIME

Listening
Time

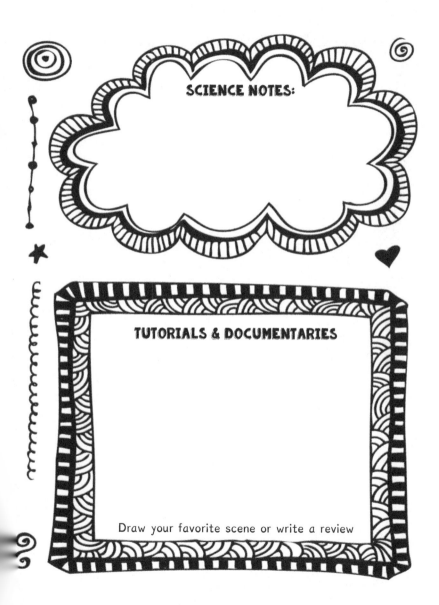

SCIENCE NOTES:

TUTORIALS & DOCUMENTARIES

Draw your favorite scene or write a review

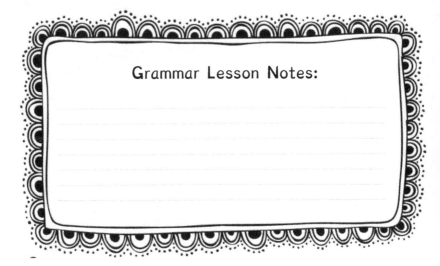

Grammar Lesson Notes:

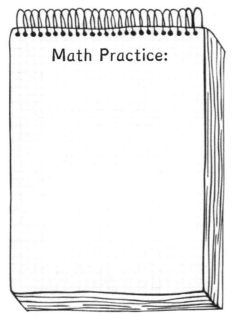

Math Practice:

Spelling Words:

Make your Own Flash Cards (Front)

Make your Own Flash Cards (Back)

READING TIME

Spend time reading from all your books!

Copy your favorite paragraph:

Notes

Title:_____ Page Number_____

START YOUR DAY!

DATE:

_____

Today's News:

Nature Study

Draw something that God made.

Draw the Weather

To-Do List:

1.
2.
3.
4.

How are you feeling today?

Bible Study Time

Prayer List:

1.
2.
3.
4.
5.

Today's Bible Reading:

Bible Notes:

How can I serve others today?

Write a Bible Verse:

LEARN OR PRACTICE A SKILL

Goals:

Accomplishments:

MUSIC TIME

Listening
Time

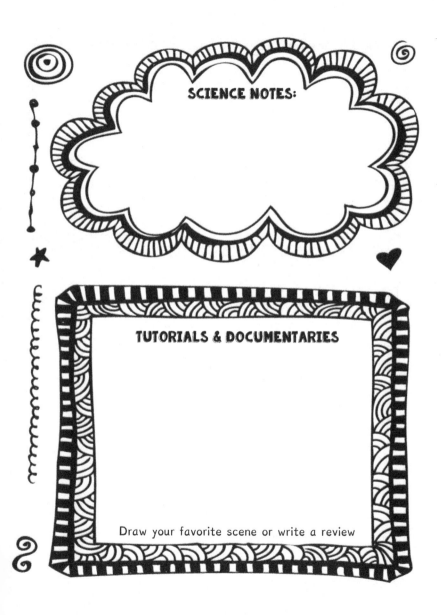

SCIENCE NOTES:

TUTORIALS & DOCUMENTARIES

Draw your favorite scene or write a review

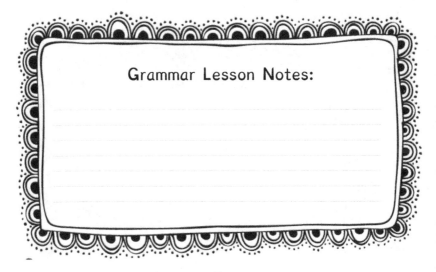

Grammar Lesson Notes:

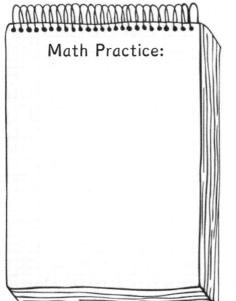

Math Practice:

Spelling Words:

Make your Own Flash Cards (Front)

Make your Own Flash Cards (Back)

READING TIME

Spend time reading from all your books!

Copy your favorite paragraph:

Notes

Title:_____ Page Number_____

CREATIVE JOURNALING

Write a Poem, Song, Scripture or Story

START YOUR DAY!

DATE:

_____

Today's News:

Nature Study

Draw something that God made.

Draw the Weather

To-Do List:

1.
2.
3.
4.

How are you feeling today?

Bible Study Time

Prayer List:

1.
2.
3.
4.
5.

Today's Bible Reading:

Bible Notes:

How can I serve others today?

Write a Bible Verse:

LEARN OR PRACTICE A SKILL

Goals:

Accomplishments:

MUSIC TIME

Listening
Time

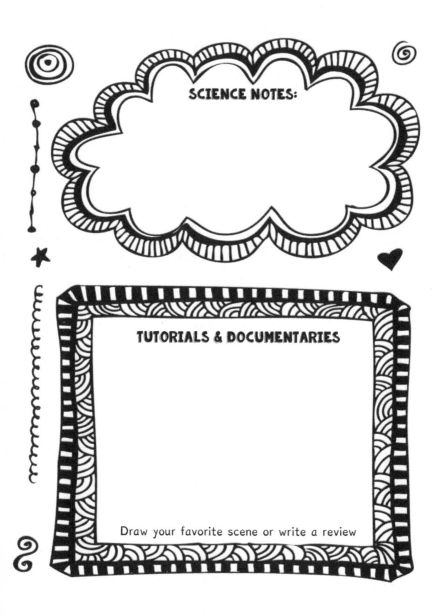

SCIENCE NOTES:

TUTORIALS & DOCUMENTARIES

Draw your favorite scene or write a review

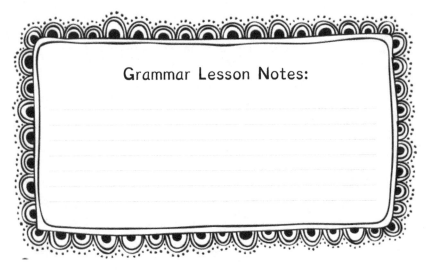

Grammar Lesson Notes:

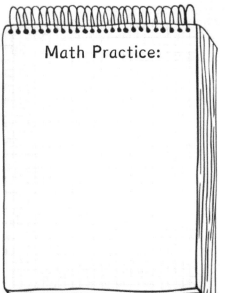

Math Practice:

Spelling Words:

Make your Own Flash Cards (Front)

Make your Own Flash Cards (Back)

READING TIME

Spend time reading from all your books!

Copy your favorite paragraph:

Notes

Title:_____ Page Number_____

II

CREATIVE JOURNALING

Write a Poem, Song, Scripture or Story

START YOUR DAY!

DATE:

_____

Today's News:

Nature Study

Draw something that God made.

Draw the Weather

To-Do List:

1.
2.
3.
4.

How are you feeling today?

Bible Study Time

Prayer List:

1.
2.
3.
4.
5.

Today's Bible Reading:

Bible Notes:

How can I serve others today?

Write a Bible Verse

LEARN OR PRACTICE A SKILL

Goals:

Accomplishments:

MUSIC TIME

Listening
Time

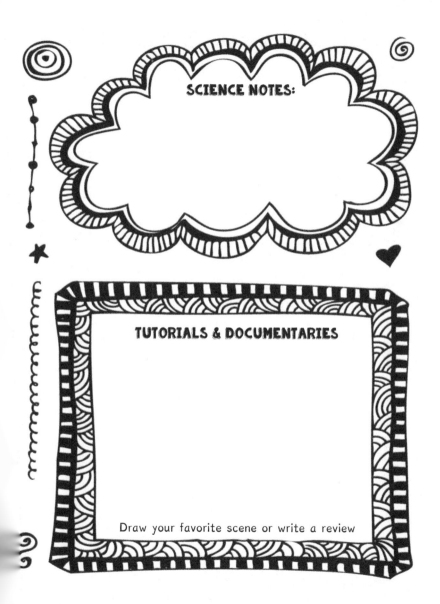

SCIENCE NOTES:

TUTORIALS & DOCUMENTARIES

Draw your favorite scene or write a review

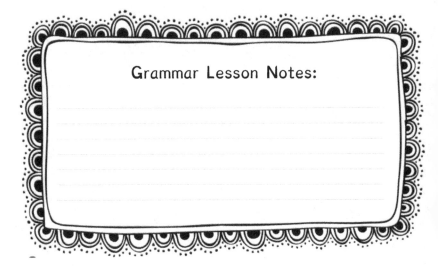

Grammar Lesson Notes:

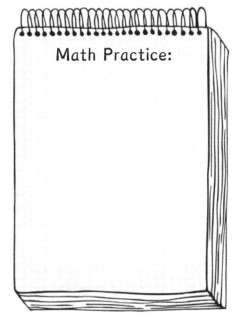

Math Practice:

Spelling Words:

Make your Own Flash Cards (Front)

Make your Own Flash Cards (Back)

READING TIME

Spend time reading from all your books!
Copy your favorite paragraph:

Notes

Title:_____ Page Number_____

Illustra

CREATIVE JOURNALING

Write a Poem, Song, Scripture or Story

START YOUR DAY!

DATE:

_____

Today's News:

Nature Study

Draw something that God made.

Draw the Weather

To-Do List:

1.
2.
3.
4.

How are you feeling today?

Bible Study Time

Prayer List:

1.
2.
3.
4.
5.

Today's Bible Reading:

Bible Notes:

How can I serve others today?

Write a Bible Verse:

LEARN OR PRACTICE A SKILL

Goals:

Accomplishments:

MUSIC TIME

Listening
Time

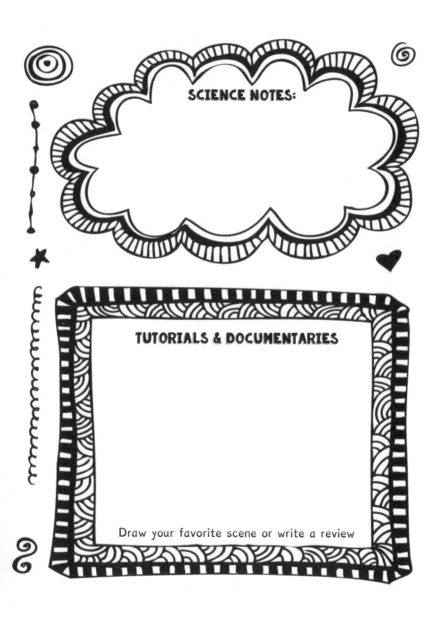

SCIENCE NOTES:

TUTORIALS & DOCUMENTARIES

Draw your favorite scene or write a review

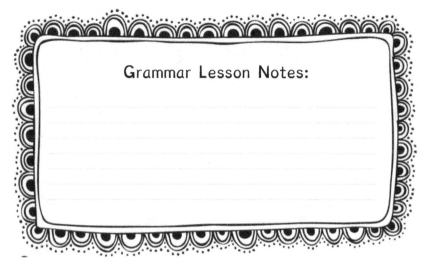

Grammar Lesson Notes:

Spelling Words:

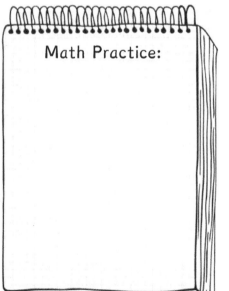

Math Practice:

Make your Own Flash Cards (Front)

Make your Own Flash Cards (Back)

READING TIME

Spend time reading from all your books!
Copy your favorite paragraph:

Notes

Title:_____ Page Number_____

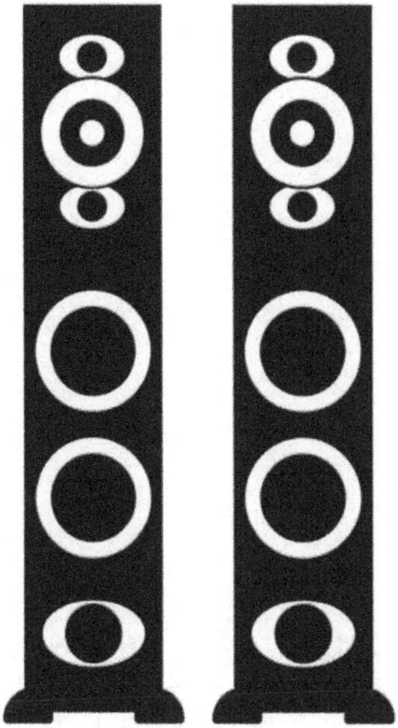

CREATIVE JOURNALING

Write a Poem, Song, Scripture or Story

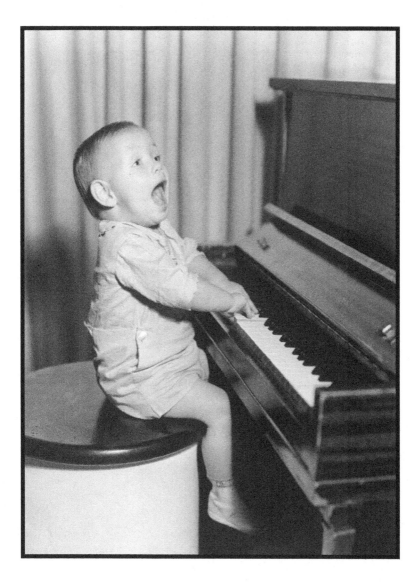

START YOUR DAY!

DATE:

_____

Today's News:

Nature Study

Draw something that God made.

Draw the Weather

To-Do List:
1.
2.
3.
4.

How are you feeling today?

Bible Study Time

Prayer List:

1.
2.
3.
4.
5.

Today's Bible Reading:

Bible Notes:

How can I serve others today?

Write a Bible Verse:

LEARN OR PRACTICE A SKILL

Goals:

Accomplishments:

MUSIC TIME

Listening
Time

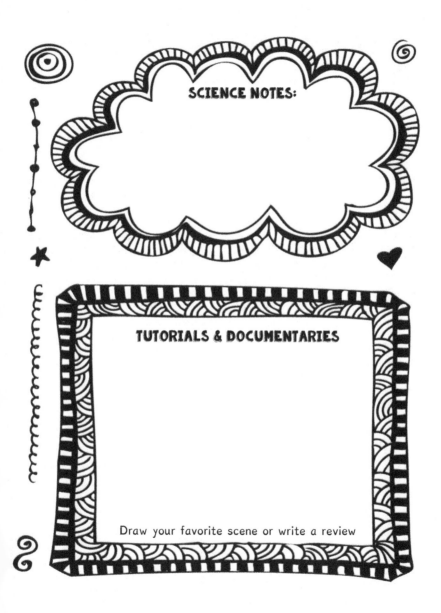

SCIENCE NOTES:

TUTORIALS & DOCUMENTARIES

Draw your favorite scene or write a review

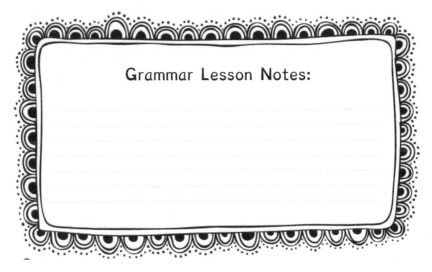

Grammar Lesson Notes:

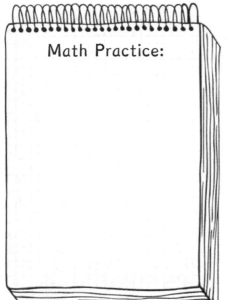

Math Practice:

Spelling Words:

Make your Own Flash Cards (Front)

Make your Own Flash Cards (Back)

READING TIME

Spend time reading from all your books!
Copy your favorite paragraph:

Notes

Title:_____ Page Number_____

CREATIVE JOURNALING

Write a Poem, Song, Scripture or Story

START YOUR DAY!

DATE:

_____

Today's News:

Nature Study

Draw something that God made.

Draw the Weather

To-Do List:

1.
2.
3.
4.

How are you feeling today?

Bible Study Time

Prayer List:

1.
2.
3.
4.
5.

Today's Bible Reading:

Bible Notes:

How can I serve others today?

Write a Bible Verse:

LEARN OR PRACTICE A SKILL

Goals:

Accomplishments:

MUSIC TIME

Listening
Time

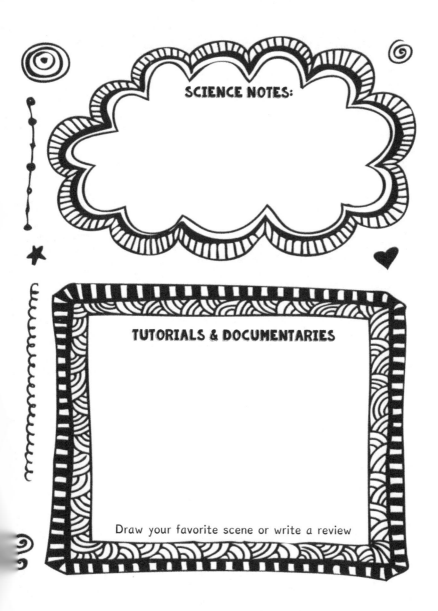

SCIENCE NOTES:

TUTORIALS & DOCUMENTARIES

Draw your favorite scene or write a review

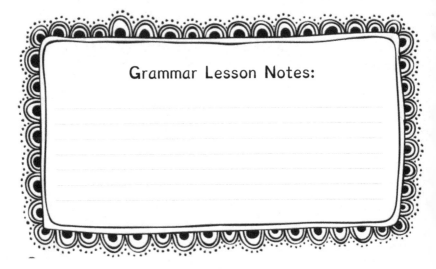

Grammar Lesson Notes:

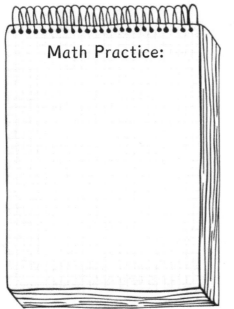

Math Practice:

Spelling Words:

Make your Own Flash Cards (Front)

Make your Own Flash Cards (Back)

READING TIME

Spend time reading from all your books!
Copy your favorite paragraph:

Notes

Title:_____ Page Number_____

CREATIVE JOURNALING

Write a Poem, Song, Scripture or Story

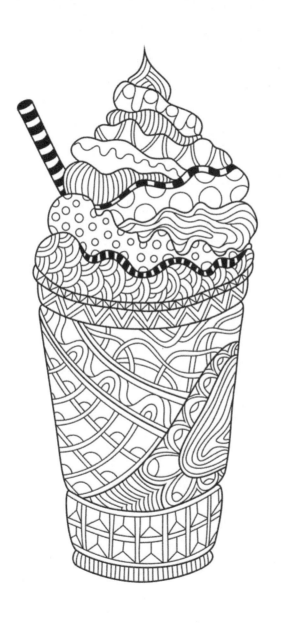

START YOUR DAY!

DATE:

_____

Today's News:

Nature Study

Draw something that God made.

Draw the Weather

To-Do List:

1.

2.

3.

4.

How are you feeling today?

Bible Study Time

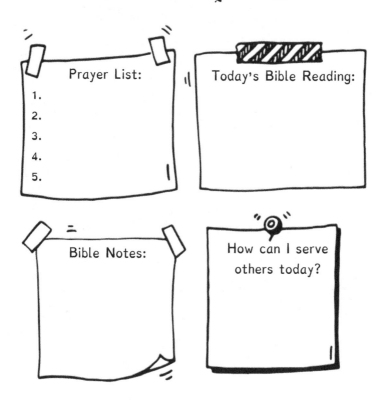

Prayer List:

1.
2.
3.
4.
5.

Today's Bible Reading:

Bible Notes:

How can I serve others today?

Write a Bible Verse:

LEARN OR PRACTICE A SKILL

Goals:

Accomplishments:

MUSIC TIME

Listening
Time

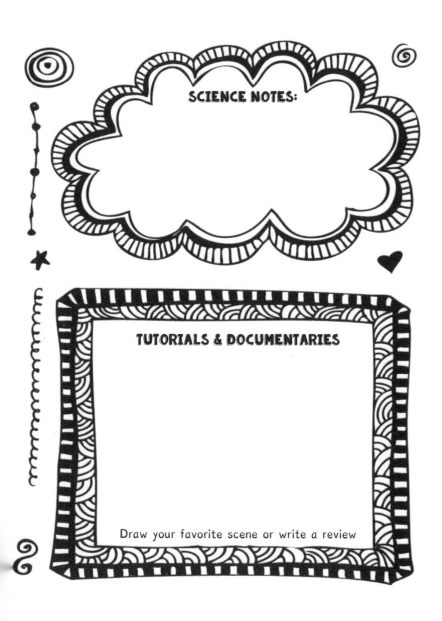

SCIENCE NOTES:

TUTORIALS & DOCUMENTARIES

Draw your favorite scene or write a review

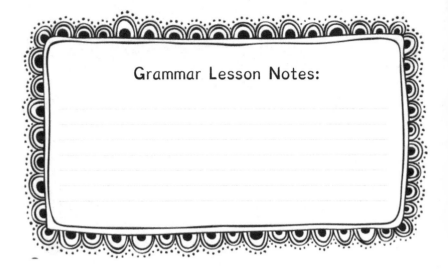

Grammar Lesson Notes:

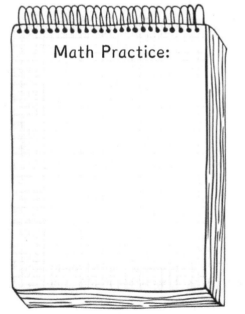

Math Practice:

Spelling Words:

Make your Own Flash Cards (Front)

Make your Own Flash Cards (Back)

READING TIME

Spend time reading from all your books!

Copy your favorite paragraph:

Notes

Title:_____ Page Number_____

Illustrate It

CREATIVE JOURNALING

Write a Poem, Song, Scripture or Story

START YOUR DAY!

DATE:

_____

Today's News:

Nature Study

Draw something that God made.

Draw the Weather

To-Do List:

1.
2.
3.
4.

How are you feeling today?

Bible Study Time

Prayer List:

1.
2.
3.
4.
5.

Today's Bible Reading:

Bible Notes:

How can I serve others today?

Write a Bible Verse:

LEARN OR PRACTICE A SKILL

Goals:

Accomplishments:

MUSIC TIME

Listening
Time

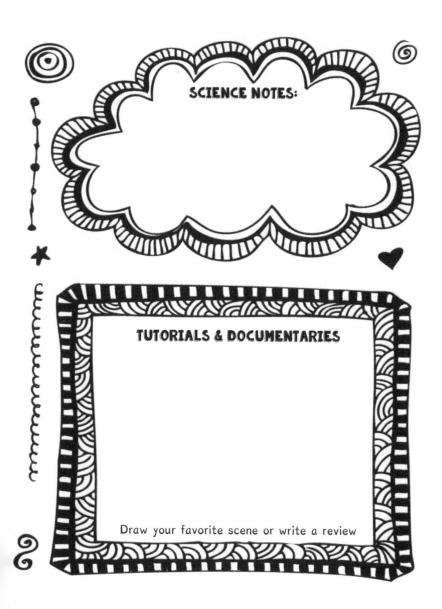

SCIENCE NOTES:

TUTORIALS & DOCUMENTARIES

Draw your favorite scene or write a review

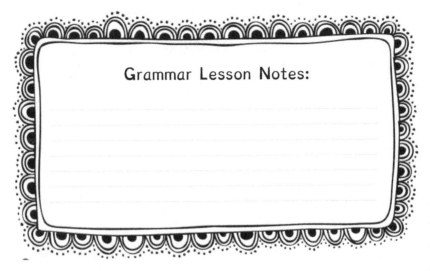

Grammar Lesson Notes:

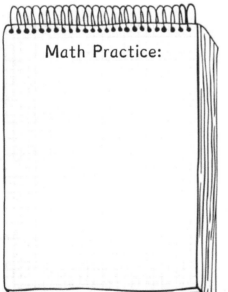

Math Practice:

Spelling Words:

Make your Own Flash Cards (Front)

Make your Own Flash Cards (Back)

READING TIME

Spend time reading from all your books!
Copy your favorite paragraph:

Notes

Title:_____ Page Number_____

CREATIVE JOURNALING

Write a Poem, Song, Scripture or Story

START YOUR DAY!

DATE:
_____
Today's News:

Nature Study

Draw something that God made.

Draw the Weather

To-Do List:
1.
2.
3.
4.

How are you feeling today?

Bible Study Time

Prayer List:

1.
2.
3.
4.
5.

Today's Bible Reading:

Bible Notes:

How can I serve others today?

Write a Bible Verse:

LEARN OR PRACTICE A SKILL

Goals:

Accomplishments:

MUSIC TIME

Listening
Time

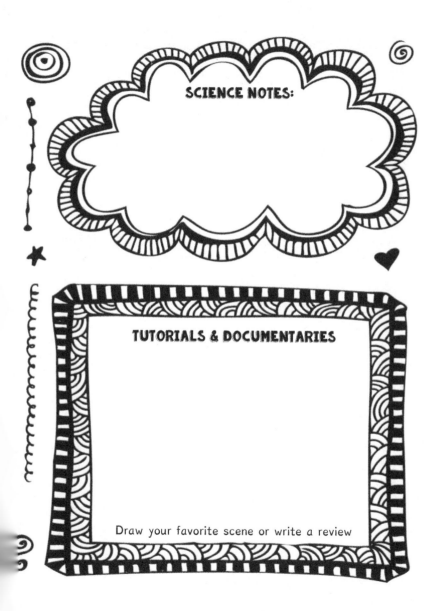

SCIENCE NOTES:

TUTORIALS & DOCUMENTARIES

Draw your favorite scene or write a review

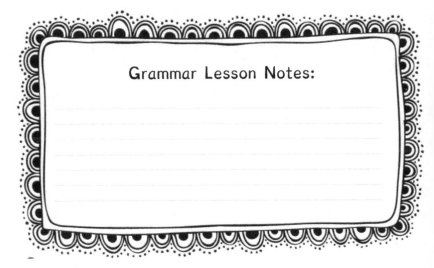

Grammar Lesson Notes:

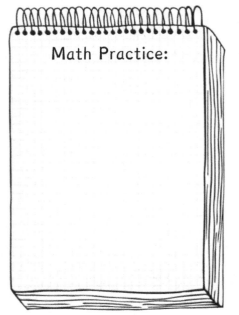

Math Practice:

Spelling Words:

Make your Own Flash Cards (Front)

Make your Own Flash Cards (Back)

READING TIME

Spend time reading from all your books!

Copy your favorite paragraph:

Notes

Title:_____ Page Number_____

CREATIVE JOURNALING

Write a Poem, Song, Scripture or Story

START YOUR DAY!

DATE:

_____

Today's News:

Nature Study

Draw something that God made.

Draw the Weather

To-Do List:

1.
2.
3.
4.

How are you feeling today?

Bible Study Time

Prayer List:

1.
2.
3.
4.
5.

Today's Bible Reading:

Bible Notes:

How can I serve others today?

Write a Bible Verse:

LEARN OR PRACTICE A SKILL

Goals:

Accomplishments:

MUSIC TIME

Listening
Time

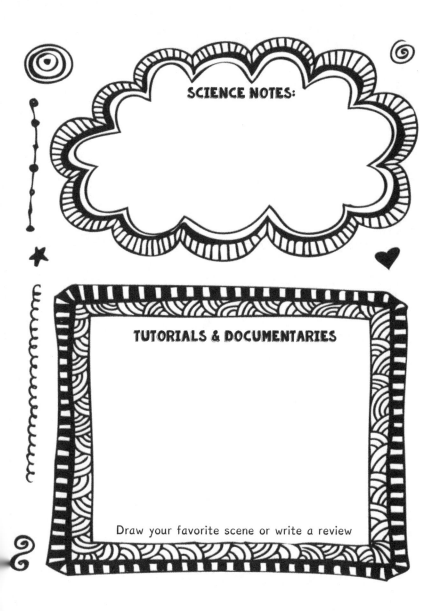

SCIENCE NOTES:

TUTORIALS & DOCUMENTARIES

Draw your favorite scene or write a review

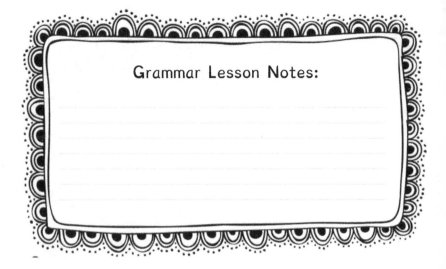

Grammar Lesson Notes:

Spelling Words:

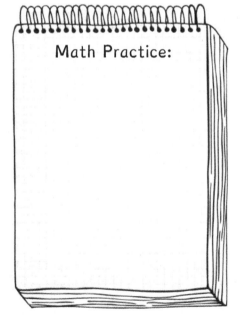

Math Practice:

Make your Own Flash Cards (Front)

Make your Own Flash Cards (Back)

READING TIME

Spend time reading from all your books!

Copy your favorite paragraph:

Notes

Title:_____ Page Number_____

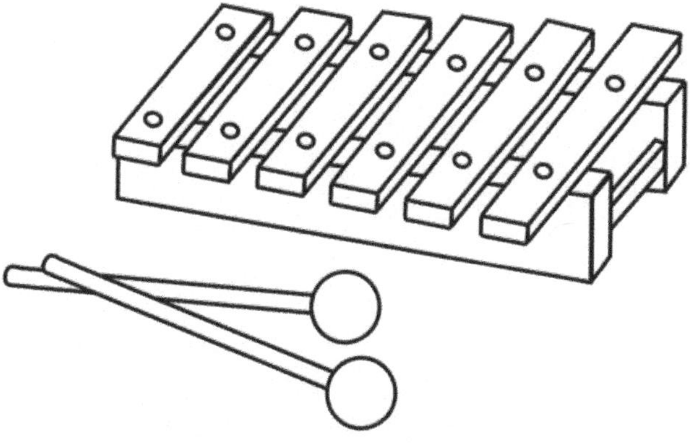

CREATIVE JOURNALING

Write a Poem, Song, Scripture or Story

START YOUR DAY!

DATE:
_____

Today's News:

Nature Study

Draw something that God made.

Draw the Weather

To-Do List:

1.
2.
3.
4.

How are you feeling today?

Bible Study Time

Prayer List:

1.
2.
3.
4.
5.

Today's Bible Reading:

Bible Notes:

How can I serve others today?

Write a Bible Verse:

LEARN OR PRACTICE A SKILL

Goals:

Accomplishments:

MUSIC TIME

Listening
Time

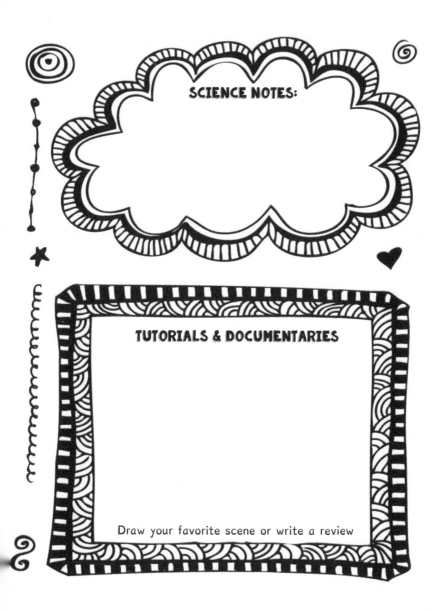

SCIENCE NOTES:

TUTORIALS & DOCUMENTARIES

Draw your favorite scene or write a review

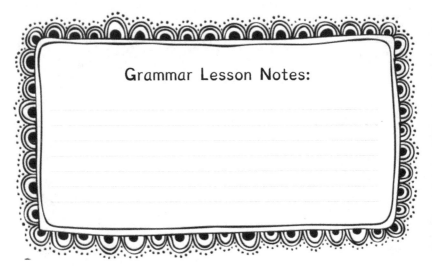

Grammar Lesson Notes:

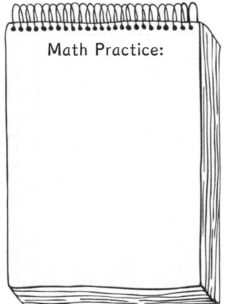

Math Practice:

Spelling Words:

Make your Own Flash Cards (Front)

Make your Own Flash Cards (Back)

READING TIME

Spend time reading from all your books!

Copy your favorite paragraph:

Notes

Title:_____ Page Number_____

_____
_____
_____
_____
_____
_____
_____
_____
_____
_____
_____
_____
_____
_____

CREATIVE JOURNALING

Write a Poem, Song, Scripture or Story

START YOUR DAY!

DATE:

_____

Today's News:

Nature Study

Draw something that God made.

Draw the Weather

To-Do List:

1.
2.
3.
4.

How are you feeling today?

Bible Study Time

Prayer List:

1.
2.
3.
4.
5.

Today's Bible Reading:

Bible Notes:

How can I serve others today?

Write a Bible Verse:

LEARN OR PRACTICE A SKILL

Goals:

Accomplishments:

MUSIC TIME

Listening
Time

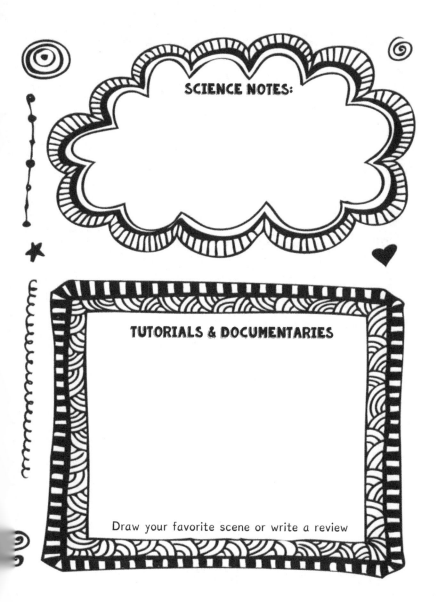

SCIENCE NOTES:

TUTORIALS & DOCUMENTARIES

Draw your favorite scene or write a review

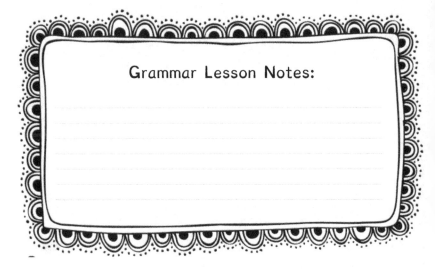

Grammar Lesson Notes:

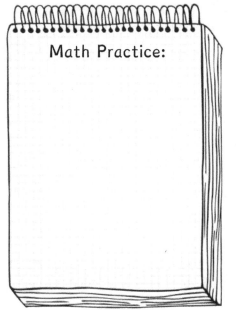

Math Practice:

Spelling Words:

Make your Own Flash Cards (Front)

Make your Own Flash Cards (Back)

READING TIME

Spend time reading from all your books!
Copy your favorite paragraph:

Notes

Title:_____ Page Number_____

Write a Bible Verse

My Books

My Books

My Books

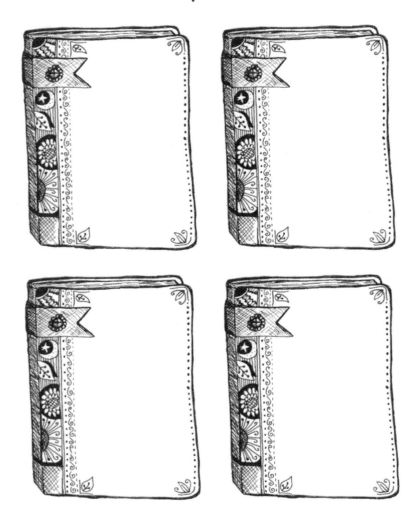

My Books

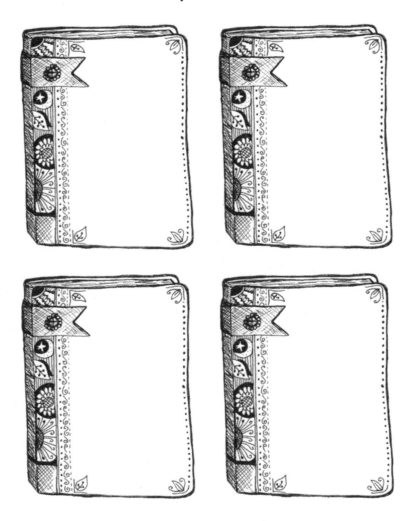

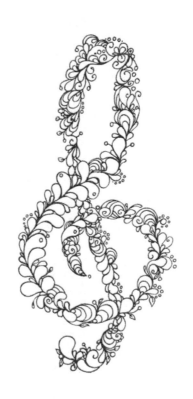

Do It Yourself
HOMESCHOOL
JOURNALS

Copyright Information

Contact Us:

The Thinking Tree LLC
317.622.8852 PHONE (Dial +1 outside of the USA)
267.712.7889 FAX

FunSchoolingBooks.com

Made in United States
Orlando, FL
08 June 2023

33914647R00225